A Place Called Brighton

Karen Leigh Kelly

Copyright © 2021 by Karen Leigh Kelly

All rights reserved. No part of this publication may be reproduced, distributed or transmitted in any form or by any means, including photocopying, recording or other electronic or mechanical methods, without the prior written permission of the author, except in the case of brief quotations embodied in reviews and certain other non-commercial uses permitted by copyright law.

Printed in the United States of America

ISBN: 978-1-953910-66-0 (hardcover)
ISBN: 978-1-953910-65-3 (paperback)
ISBN: 978-1-953910-67-7 (ebook)

Canoe Tree Press

4697 Main Street
Manchester Center, VT 05255

Canoe Tree Press is a division of DartFrog Books.

To my father, Dr. Claude Kelso Kelly.

As a young country doctor, he purchased the property known as Brighton in King William County, Virginia, in 1952. He believed it would be an ideal place to live and raise his family. Throughout his life, he modeled empathy and skill in caring for others. As a father, he instilled a deep respect for history and a passion for opportunities that furthered the best in everyone.

Figure 2. Karen and her father, Dr. Claude Kelso Kelly, in the living room at Brighton, January 1956. (Photo: Kelly family archive)

About the Author

Figure 3. The author, Karen Kelly (center), and her family in the Organ Mountains-Desert Peaks National Monument, Las Cruces, New Mexico, December 2019. (Source: Devin Hume)

Karen Leigh Kelly, an educational consultant, divides her time between homes in New Mexico and Greece. She is one of four surviving siblings who share vivid memories of growing up at Brighton. Born in 1955, Karen lived on Brighton farm in King William County, Virginia, with her parents, Claude and Nettie, and her "Irish twin brother", Claude, Jr. (Kelso), who is ten months older. A sister, Paula, followed in 1956, and twins, Earl and David, in 1961. Karen's love of her Virginia home, Brighton, has deepened over the years, even as she moved to Colorado to attend college. In 1995, she earned a doctoral degree at the University of Denver and enjoyed many years as a university professor. In 1999 she received a Fulbright Scholar appointment to Cyprus to develop educational programs. From 2004 to 2019 she served as contributing faculty for Walden University while also advising state and international educational organizations, including the Department of Education in Colorado; the Supreme Education Council in Qatar; the Aga Khan Development Foundation, based in France; the World Bank, based in Washington, DC; and the Early Childhood Authority in the UAE. She and her husband, Jock, live near the Organ Mountains-Desert Peaks National Monument in Las Cruces, New Mexico, where they enjoy hiking the extensive network of BLM trails. As often as possible, they visit their extended family in Virginia, as well as their five adult children and spouses, and seven grandchildren who live in Colorado, Hawaii, Nevada, and North Dakota.

Contents

Introduction: Brighton 1750–2021 9
Chapter I: Brighton and Native American Lands 17
Chapter II: Brighton, One of Virginia's Oldest Plantation Homes 25
Chapter III: Chronology of "Brighton" Owners 1786–1854 47
Chapter IV: Brighton: The War Years, Reconstruction, and the
    20th Century 1855 to 1952 65
Chapter V: Brighton, the Most Recent Years 1952 to 2021 89
Photo Epilogue: The Kelly Family at Brighton 153
List of Figures 177
Bibliography 185

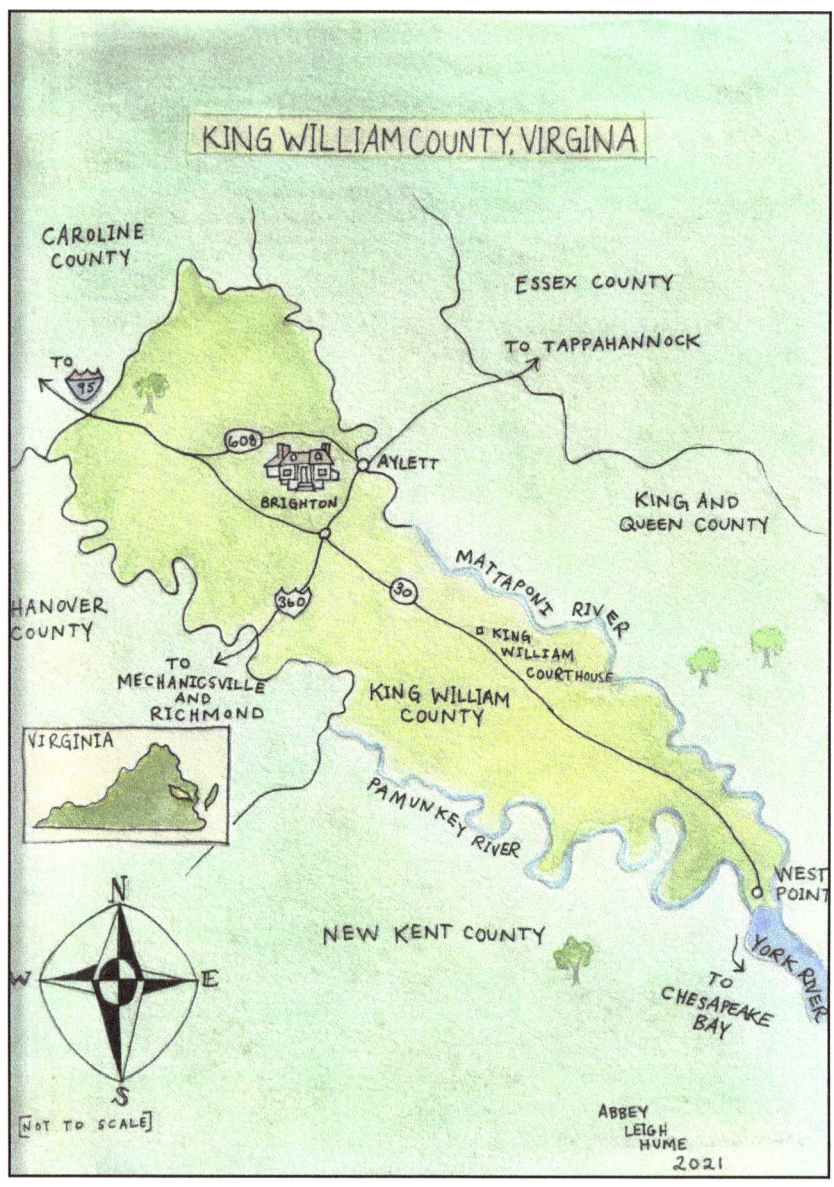

Figure 4. Location of Brighton on Map of King William County, Virginia (Source: Abbey Leigh Hume 2021)

INTRODUCTION
Brighton 1750-2021

Figure 5. Brighton Farm in King William County, Virginia, 2020. (Source: The Steele Group Sotheby's International Realty)

My childhood home, Brighton, has a distinctive history that originated in the seventeenth century, about the time that English settlers established the first colonies along the eastern shores of the United States. Constructed in 1750[1], this historic home and property were part of a large land grant and likely named after a town of the same name along the southern coast of England. Today, the property known as Brighton lies three miles from the Mattaponi River Bridge in Aylett, Virginia, in King William County. This rural county, in the eastern region of Virginia, covers 275 square miles and supports a population of sixteen thousand residents. Visitors can find Brighton by turning west off of Virginia State Route 360 in Aylett and following the tree-lined County Route 608, also known as the old road from Aylett to Mangohick (See Figure 4).

Known as a Southern Colonial home, and one of the oldest in the area, Brighton has maintained its charm and character for close to three centuries. If the Georgian structure could speak, it would tell stories of the local Native American tribes, the conflicts that led to the American Revolution, the Southern perspective of the Civil War (aka the War Between the States *or* the War of Northern Aggression, depending on whom you ask), enslaved and free Black people's perspective on the same (aka the Freedom War), the Reconstruction era, the Wall Street crash of 1929, two world wars, segregation, the civil rights movement, the dawn of space exploration, and so much more.

Figure 6. The Lane and Bullheads by Sotheby's. The bullheads on the brick pillars were salvaged from a demolished bank building in Richmond, VA. Eva Jo and Claude Kelly purchased two as gifts for each other on their first anniversary. Eva Jo painted them black to resemble the Black Angus herd at Brighton. (Source: The Steele Group Sotheby's International Realty)

County records show that Brighton has been bought and sold many times over the past few centuries. The current property comprises 306 acres, which include eighty acres of cultivated fields; a 3,000 square foot prerevolutionary home; several well-kept outbuildings, including a studio apartment and a farm shop; and a ten-acre, spring-fed bass pond. When turning off the narrow, paved road, now known as Upshaw Road, onto the sandy graveled lane, visitors to Brighton pass between two life-sized Black Angus stone bullheads mounted on red brick pillars. The lane proceeds about a quarter of a mile to the main house, through fields of neon-green winter wheat, or rows of corn or soybeans, depending on the season.

Figure 7. Black Angus Bullhead at the end of the lane leading to Brighton. (Source: Kelly family archive)

Details about the original builders, owners, and land transactions involving Brighton have proven challenging to trace because of the destruction and loss of legal documents and records in New Kent, King and Queen, and King William counties.[2] Birth, death, and marriage certificates and land deeds were among the many records destroyed in three devastating fires at the King William County Courthouse in 1787, 1864, and 1885.[3] Despite these fires, the King William County Courthouse, constructed in 1725, remains the oldest courthouse building still in use in the United States.

Further complicating these genealogical challenges, King William County is one of eighteen Virginia counties that lost all their 1790 and 1810 US Census data in 1814 when British troops torched public buildings in Washington, DC, toward the end of the War of 1812. Fortunately, extracts from King William County tax and personal property lists provide clues to the many owners of Brighton and the neighboring properties, beginning in 1782 when such lists became available.[4]

Figure 8. The King William County Courthouse is the oldest courthouse still in continuous use in the United States. (Source: Eugene Campbell)

Figure 9. The King William County Courthouse, built in 1725, has survived several devastating fires resulting in the loss of many early land deeds and legal documents. (Source: Eugene Campbell)

Additionally, nineteen volumes of county records, with over eight thousand documents dating back to 1702, once thought destroyed, were discovered in old boxes under floorboards when the King William County clerk transferred offices to an adjacent building in 2004. These lost records have been digitized and made available in their partially burnt, original form (See Figure 10) on flash drives from the King William County Historical Society of Virginia.[5] The following narrative results from an extensive review of the owners of Brighton from the eighteenth century to the present day, gleaned from these recovered fragments and research published by historians. I hope that this review will be informative to the casual reader and serve as a resource for anyone interested in knowing a little more about A Place Called Brighton.

Figure 10. This recovered Deed Book was one of many that were salvaged following devastating fires at the King William County Courthouse. (Source: King William County Historical Society)

Figure 11. The house at Brighton as seen from the ten-acre pond on the southern boundary of the property. (Source: Karen Kelly)

1. Pearson, Sally, Commissioner of Revenue. (2014) *King William County Property Assessment.*
2. McMillan, Jackson. (January 7, 2015) "Historian tracks down original King William County documents dating back to 1702." *TidewaterReview.*https://www.dailypress.com/tidewater-review/va-tr-byline-kw-historical-society-documents-0107-20150106-story.html
3. Edwards, Bibb. (2012) *Our Courthouse Fires.* King William County Historical Society.
4. Library of Virginia (2017) *Lost Records Localities: Counties and Cities with Missing Records.* Research Notes Number 30. https://www.lva.virginia.gov/public/guides/rn30_lostrecords.pdf
5. King William County Historical Society. http://kingwilliamhistory.org/category/kwchs-projects/page/2/

CHAPTER I
Brighton and Native American Lands

"In elementary school I had to memorize all of the counties in Virginia and identify them on a state map. Each county was considered an important part of Virginia history. Even today, if you ask a Virginian where they are from, they will tell you the county, rather than the town or city. This early lesson in geography instilled a desire in me to explore beyond boundaries and to really 'see' how the world fits together."

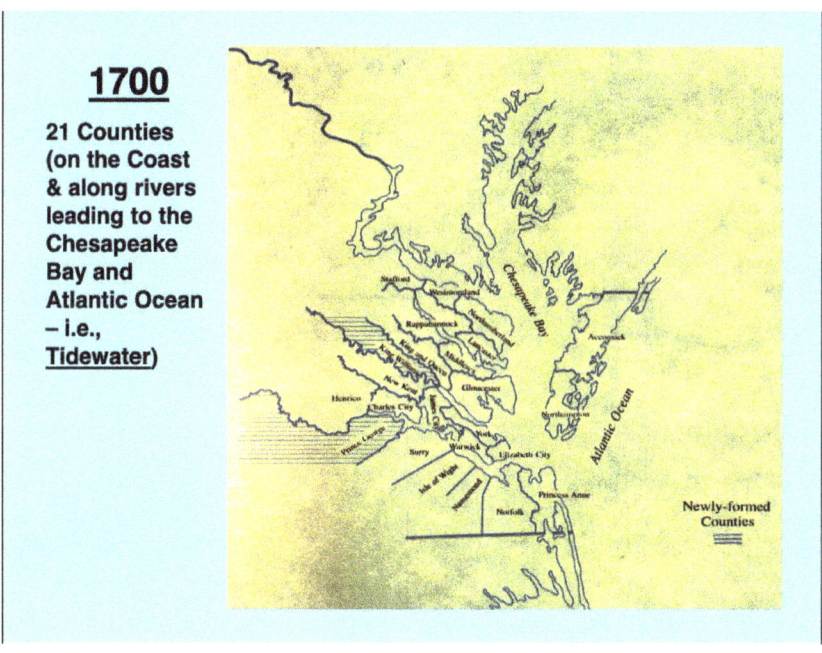

Figure 12. . Location of newly formed counties in Virginia in 1700 (Source: Virginia History Series 2007)[1]

The land surrounding Brighton lies within the banks of the Pamunkey and Mattaponi Rivers in the Tidewater region of Virginia. Native American tribes and early settlers referred to the area as the

"Pamunkey Neck." Also known as the Upper Mattaponi in colonial times, the region was part of New Kent County, which lies to the southwest. In 1691, the English designated this area as part of King and Queen County, which occupies the northeastern side of the Mattaponi.

By 1702, the entire region between the two rivers, which merge to form the York River at the town of West Point, became King William County. The colonists named the county in honor of King William III (William of Orange), the king of England, Scotland, and Ireland from 1689 to 1702. In 1720 and 1727, the uppermost western regions of King William County were redistributed to form parts of Spotsylvania and Caroline Counties, respectively. Before the establishment of these counties, the lands that became included in the property known as Brighton bordered the hunting and fishing grounds of a local Native American tribe, the Mattaponi, or the "people of the river."[2] Mattaponi translated means "landing place." The tribe originated as a branch of the Pamunkey and Chickahominy tribes, who lived along Virginia's waterways. The Virginia Department of Education (VDOE) offers the following description of the Mattaponi people, a core tribe under Chief Powhatan, who, for many years, lived within the Chickahominy tribe:

> "For centuries the Upper Mattaponi People lived in villages along the waterways of Virginia. They lived in union with the land, the first farmers of America, harvesting corn, beans and squash and hunting deer in ways still employed today. Like their neighboring tribes, they spoke the Algonquian language and when the British came in 1607; they were prosperous people under the leadership of Chief Powhatan, the Paramount Chief of over 30 neighboring tribes. Bacon's rebellion of 1676 led to the Peace Treaty of 1677, signed on behalf of the Mattaponi by Werowansqua Cockacoeske, Queen of the Pamunkey, and a reservation of Chickahominy Indians and some of the Mattaponi Indians was established near the village site of Passaunkack".[3]

Figure 13. Cockacoeske, chief of the Pamunkey Indian Tribe (1640-1686) for thirty years, maintained peace and unity among the tribes in the Tidewater region of Virginia. (Source: Wikimedia Commons)[4]

While historians are uncertain of the exact location of the settlement of Passaunkack, the village occupied both sides of the Mattaponi River, including the current towns of Walkerton and Aylett. A 1612 map (see Figure 14), drawn by Captain John Smith, and a 1670/1673 map drawn by August Hermann (see Figure 15), shows a large concentration of Indians living in a village called Passaunkack, near the present town of Aylett about three miles from Brighton.

Figure 14. An early map of Virginia created by Captain John Smith in 1612. (Source: Library of Virginia)[5]

Figure 15. This map by August Hermann in 1673 shows the location of Indian villages near the Mattaponi River in an area later established as King William County, Virginia. (Source: Library of Congress)[6]

Following repeated altercations, including search and destroy raids, burning of villages and crops, and other atrocities committed by the encroaching colonists and the Native Americans, both parties signed a treaty in 1677. Known as the Treaty of Middle Plantation, the agreement restricted planters from settling within three miles of any Indian town. A map of reservation lands in 1702 shows that the Mattaponi reservation covered a large settlement near Aylett Creek and crossed all three branches of Herring Creek. Aylett Creek, which is south of Herring Creek, runs through the southern boundary of the current property at Brighton. In the maps below (see Figures 16 and 17), the Mattaponi reservation lies between two Herring Creek branches. Within these boundaries is the present-day Upshaw Road and the current Brighton property, as indicated by the ten-acre pond, which is fed by Aylett Creek, built in 1958 by Brighton owner Dr. Claude K. Kelly. Indian arrowheads have been found on the property by the Kelly children as late as the 1960s. In 1698, this section of Chickahominy/Mattaponi tribal land *"was described as being located between the two Herring Creeks, probably the streams known as Aylett and Herring/Dorrell Creeks."*[7]

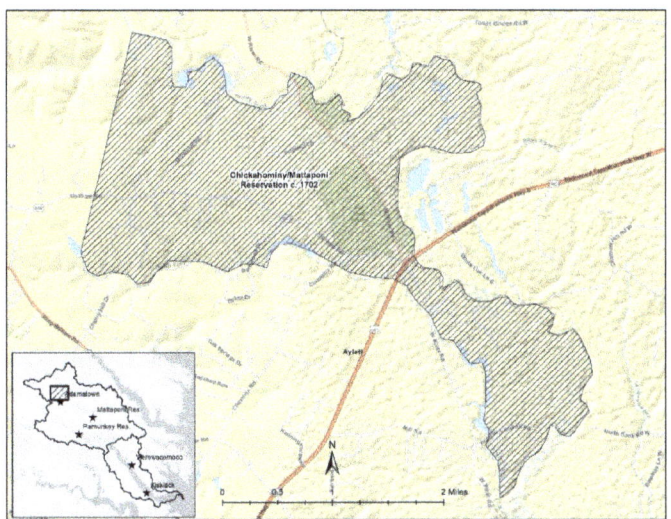

Figure 32. Chickahominy/Mattaponi reservation, between "two Herring creeks."

Figure 16. Chickahominy/Mattaponi reservation, between the Herring Creeks. (Source: Strickland, King and McCartney)

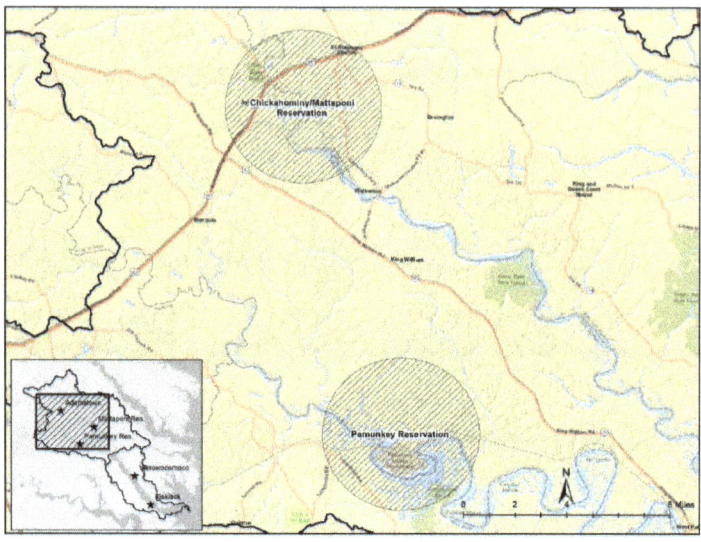

Figure 31. Three-mile buffer Native reservations, pre-1705.

Figure 17. Three-mile buffer zone of Mattaponi Village near present-day Aylett, Virginia. (Source: Strickland, King and McCartney)[8]

Thus, while the land surrounding Brighton may have been granted to English colonists in the late seventeenth century, it was a hostile environment for planters until after 1705 when the Mattaponi people were displaced because of the increasing encroachment of colonists.[9] As of 2020, about seventy-five of the 450 descendants of the Mattaponi tribe still live in King William County on one of the oldest reservations in the United States. The reservation, established in 1658, occupies land long held by the tribe along the Mattaponi River, about twelve miles from Brighton. The tribe is state-recognized and continues to maintain its own government and fulfill its treaty obligations set forth in 1646.[10]

1. Virginia History Series #607 (2007). *Life, Growth & Development in the Virginia Colonies (1700–1760). 21 Counties.* Slide 4 http://virginiahistoryseries.org/linked/unit%206.%20life.growth.development%20of%20va%20colony.slides.pdf.
2. Official Site of the Mattaponi Indian Reservation, https://www.mattaponination.com/history.html
3. Virginia Department of Education. *Virginia's First People: Upper Mattaponi Indian Tribe* http://www.doe.virginia.gov/instruction/history/virginias-first-people/today/upper-mattaponi/index.shtml
4. Kss5pj, CC BY-SA 4.0 <https://creativecommons.org/licenses/by-sa/4.0>, via Wikimedia Commons. Wikimedia Commons contributors, "File: Cockacoeske VWM Statue.jpg," *Wikimedia Commons, the free media repository*, https://commons.wikimedia.org/w/index.php?title=File:Cockacoeske_VWM_Statue.jpg&oldid=511633488 (accessed February 2, 2021).
5. Virginia Department of Historic Resources (1610). *Virginia Discovered and Discribed: John Smith's Map of Virginia and its Derivatives.* Research Notes 28. The Library of Virginia, Richmond. https://www.lva.virginia.gov/public/guides/rn28_johnsmith.pdf.
6. Herrman, Augustine, 1621 Or, Henry Faithorne, and Thomas Withinbrook. *Virginia and Maryland as it is planted and inhabited this present year.* [London: Augustine Herrman and Thomas Withinbrook, 1673] The Library of Congress, Geography and Map Division. https://www.loc.gov/item/2002623131/.
7. McIlwaine, H. R. and Kennedy, et al. eds. (1905–1915) *Journal of the House of Burgesses.* 13 volumes. Richmond: Library of Virginia. 1695–1702, 349, 358. As cited in *Mattaponi Indian Reservation, King William County, Virginia* (October 2017). College of William & Mary Anthropological Research Report Series, n.7, and Commonwealth of Virginia Research Report Series, n. 23, p.16. https://www.pocahontaslives.com/uploads/6/7/2/9/6729327/mattaponi_research_report_for_distribution.pdf

8. Strickland, S., King, J., and McCartney, M. (2019). *Defining the Greater York River Indigenous Cultural Landscape.* (95–96) St. Mary's College of Maryland, St. Mary's City, Maryland. https://chesapeakeconservancy.org/wp-content/uploads/2020/02/York-ICL-Final.pdf
9. Strickland, King, and McCartney (2019).
10. Official Site of the Mattaponi Indian Reservation https://www.mattaponination.com/history.html

CHAPTER II
Brighton, One of Virginia's Oldest Plantation Homes

Figure 18. Living room at Brighton with pine wood floors. (Source: The Steele Group Sotheby's International Realty)

"One of my earliest memories of Brighton are of the pine wood floors. As a child I was prone to getting splinters and the removal of slivers of wood from my feet, after sliding around the polished floors, was always painful."

Over the years, historians have recounted stories of the plantation homes established in King William County, many of which still stand. Some homes have fallen into disrepair and neglect. Others damaged by fires, have been rebuilt, renovated, and modernized. Many pre-revolutionary homes built along rivers and creeks, have window and door openings at heights above the water's edge to avoid arrows from local Indians traveling in canoes. It's likely that colonists built their first homes on properties obtained through the distribution of land grants by the kings of England, beginning with James I (1603), Charles I (1625), and later William III, who was king of England, Scotland, and Ireland from 1689 to 1702.[1] These kings bestowed grants upon adventurers and planters who traveled to the colonies in the early seventeenth century to explore the new world. When the crown of England dissolved the Virginia Company of London in 1624, they offered generous land patents to any person who made the long journey to the colonies and who qualified as a planter.[2]

Research of King William County land patents conducted by historian Elizabeth Hawes Ryland in 1935, at the request of Brighton owner Mrs. Howard L. Clarke, revealed that Brighton is one of the oldest homes in the county and one of several plantations that began as a land grant. Even though her research was thorough, Ryland could not confirm the original builder or owner of Brighton. In her review of documents, she discovered tax records indicating that the tracts of land comprising the farm were within part of the original land grant of 1673 bestowed to Colonel William Byrd I, a fur trader who immigrated to Virginia from England in 1669. The land grant, which provided abundant acreage along the James River, also included rich farmland as described in painstaking detail in a land deed abstract for William Byrd dated October 23, 1703.

> 1200 acres between the Herring Creeks in King William County, beginning at the crooked white oak on the side of the bank of the Mattapony River between Yarborough's ferry and Bird's quarter farm, thence up and along the river its several courses to a red oak and a white oak at the foot of the hill by the riverside just below the mouth of a branch called little branch thence by lines of marked trees south 60 degrees West 382 poles to two white oaks thence South 28 degrees East 120 poles to 2 Spanish oaks by the side of Williams plantation thence 67 degrees East 126 poles to a great white oak thence South 45 degrees East 136 poles to a pine in an old field near White's house thence 9 degrees east 54 poles to 2 small gums by the run of Middle Herring Creek Southwest thence North 78 degrees East 192 poles to the beginning.[3]

Another reference to William Byrd's extensive property can be found in the 1704 Virginia Quit Rent Roll that listed landowners who were obligated to pay the king an annual "quit rent" of one shilling, or a comparable amount of tobacco, for every fifty acres owned. This document noted that William Byrd, Esq. owned 19,500 acres in Henrico County, 572 acres in King and Queen County, and 1,200 acres in King William County. These payments to support the crown resulted in hostility on the part of the independent colonists, who often resorted to payments made in "trash tobacco." Years later, colonists abolished the land-tenure system, along with many other British taxes, including the Stamp Act (1765) and the Tea Act (1773). Resentment about their lack of representation in Parliament soon led to the American Revolution (1775–1783) and the Declaration of Independence in 1776.[4]

Figure 19. William Byrd II (1674-1744) was an American planter considered to be the founder of Richmond, Virginia. Byrd inherited many acres of farmland in King William County that included the land surrounding Brighton. (Source: Hans Hysing - Virginia Historical Society)[5]

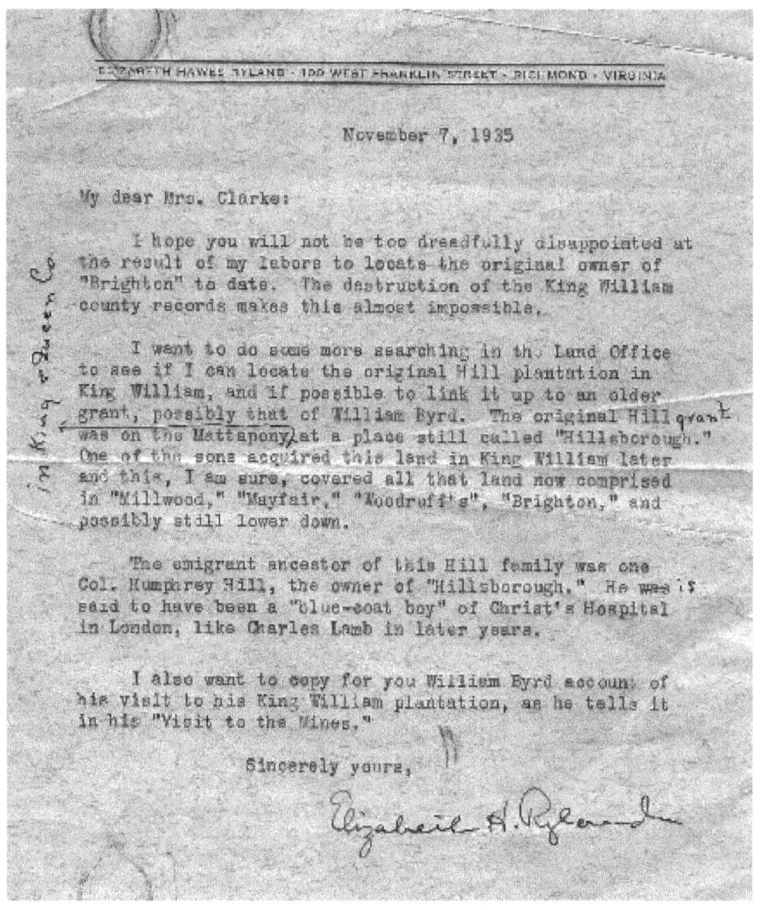

Figure 20. Letter from Elizabeth Hawes Ryland to Mrs. Howard L. Clark in 1935 regarding the results of her research on Brighton. (Source: Kelly family archive)

Colonel Byrd's son, William Byrd II (1674-1744), an American planter considered to be the founder of the city of Richmond, Virginia, inherited these farmlands from his father. Occasionally, the young William Byrd traveled to King William County from his plantation home, Westover, on the James River. There he met with overseers of the family's farms and plantations.[6] Quoted below is an account of one such visit according to entries in his detailed and colorful journal, A Progress to the Mines in the Year 1732.

7th. This morning Mrs. Martin was worse, so that there were no hopes of seeing how much she was altered. Nor was this all, but the indisposition of his consort made the colonel intolerably grave and thoughtful. I prudently ate a meat breakfast, to give me spirits for a long journey, and a long fast. My landlord was so good as to send his servant along with me, to guide me through all the turnings of a difficult way. In about four miles we crossed Mattaponi river at Norman's ford, and then slanted down to King William county road. We kept along that for about twelve miles, as far as the new brick church. After that I took a blind path, that carried me to several of Col. Jones's quarters, which border upon my own. The colonel's overseers were all abroad, which made me fearful I should find mine as idle as they. But I was mistaken, for when I came to Gravel Hall, the first of my plantations in King William, I found William Snead (that looks after three of them) very honestly about his business. I had the pleasure to see my people all well, and my business in good forwardness. I visited all the five quarters on that side, which spent so much of my time, that I had no leisure to see any of those on the other side the river; though I discoursed Thomas Tinsley, one of the overseers, who informed me how matters went. In the evening Tinsley conducted me to Mrs. Sym's house, where I intended to take up my quarters. This lady, at first suspecting I was some lover, put on a gravity that becomes a weed; but so soon as she learned who I was, brightened up into an unusual cheerfulness and serenity. She was a portly, handsome dame, of the family of Esau, and seemed not to pine too much for the death of her husband, who was of the family of the Saracens. He left a son by her, who has all the strong features of his sire, not softened in the least by any of hers, so that the most malicious of her neighbours cannot bring his legitimacy in question, not even the parson's wife, whose unruly tongue, they say, does not spare even the reverend doctor, her husband. This widow is a person of a lively and cheerful conversation, with much less reserve than most of her countrywomen. It becomes her very well and sets off her other agreeable qualities to advantage. We tossed off a bottle of honest Port, which we relished with a broiled chicken. At nine I retired to my devotions, and then slept so sound that fancy itself was stupified, else I should have dreamed of my most obliging landlady.

> 8th. I moistened my clay with a quart of milk and tea, which I found altogether as great a help to discourse as the juice of the grape. The courteous widow invited me to rest myself there that good day, and go to church with her, but I excused myself, by telling her she would certainly spoil my devotion. Then she civilly entreated me to make her house my home whenever I visited my plantations, which made me bow low, and thank her very kindly.[7]

Early tax documentation for the land surrounding Brighton was also associated with the family of British immigrant Colonel Humphrey Hill. Colonel Hill was a successful tobacco merchant who obtained property in King William County when it was still considered part of King and Queen County prior to 1702. Hill acquired property through the British "headright" system, which was one means of distributing virgin lands in the seventeenth century.[8] Similar to land grants, the British government instituted the headright system to attract English families to settle in the new colonies. This system remained in place until the Revolutionary War.[9]

The headright system offered each English colonist who qualified as a planter and anyone he transported to the colonies a plot of fifty acres per person. The land was free as long as the landowner agreed to settle and develop at least three acres of each plot of land. These plots, which became known as patents, could be inherited, traded, sold, or gifted among the colonists and their families. To receive a land patent, the patentee had to appear before a county court to present proof of expenses incurred in transporting individuals to the colonies. Colonial land office patents noted the name of the patentee, the size of the tract, the county of location, and a description of the land and date of patent signature. Copies of the patents hung on strings in the office of the Secretary of the Colony at the land office were recorded in bound volumes, as time allowed. This inefficient and often random system resulted in the occasional loss of patent documents.[10]

The early land office patents for Brighton have been challenging to locate. The Virginia State Archives hold documents of King William County tax lists dating back to 1782. These documents reveal that the descendants of the Hill family owned several properties in

King and Queen and King William Counties. Some properties on the Mattaponi River included the plantations of Hillsborough (built in 1722 by Sir Humphrey Hill and raided by the British during the American Revolution) as well as the connecting properties of Millwood, Mayfair, Woodruffe, and Brighton. The descriptions below of Brighton and the neighboring plantations of Millwood, Warsaw, Octagon, and Cownes is quoted from Ryland's research in 1935 (See Figure 23).

MILLWOOD

The old part of Millwood, that fronting the pond, was originally the miller's house belonging to the estate of Mr. John Sizer. It consisted of one large room on the first floor and a passage running through at the side; a basement room underneath; and one large and one small room above with dormer windows. When the Sizer's house at Mayfair burned, Mr. John Sizer's son, Augustus, moved with his family to Millwood. He added a room as a guest chamber and built an outside kitchen. In 1872 or '73, the house being too small for his growing family, Mr. Sizer moved the guest chamber, which was later used as a schoolhouse and now forms a part of the cottage in the yard and built an L to the original house and did away with the dormer windows. After the death of Mr. Sizer, his children being married and scattered, Mr. J.C. Fox of Ayletts bought the place and lived there until it was bought back by Ryland Sizer, a grandson of Mr. Augustus Sizer. "Millwood" at present (1935) consists of three connecting farms, "Mayfair", "Millwood" and "Duncans". The mill is still in operation and the beautiful pond furnishes good boating, swimming and fishing for the numerous guests whom Ryland often brings from New York for the weekends.

WARSAW

This house, a frame building, with bricks filling in the space between weatherboarding and laths, was the home of John Camm Pollard, brother of Robert Pollard, Jr. and his wife was Mary Ellen Chamberlayne, sister of Robert Pollard's wife. The date of the building has been determined, by the style of the architecture, in 1735. This place, with "Octagon" and "Edgehill" and "Pine Top" farms, was a part of the original Pollard estate. It was sold several times, once to James Caldwell, and once to Mr. Dunn, and finally came again to the Pollard family when bought by Robert Pollard, a grandson of Robert Pollard, Jr. of "Zoar". From him it was purchased a few years ago by Tom Peete Cross of the faculty of the University of Chicago, and his wife Elizabeth Douglas Weathers, great granddaughter of Robert Pollard, Jr. By them, the present owners, it has been carefully restored.

Figure 21. Warsaw, built circa 1770, was sold to developers in 2019. The property lies about 2 miles from Brighton on Rt. 608. Kelso and Karen Kelly took piano and guitar lessons from the owner in the mid-1960s. (Source: Long & Foster Real Estate, CVRMLS)

Octagon

As its name indicates, this house is a perfect octagon in shape, and the only one I've ever seen. The interior is wonderfully roomy for the size of the building, having two good-sized rooms on the first floor and three good bedrooms on the second. It was built about the year 1853, and was the home of James Otway Pollard, Clerk of King William after the death of his father, Robert Pollard, Jr. It is now the home of a daughter and granddaughter of James Otway Pollard, and has the reputation of being the most beautifully kept place in the neighborhood.

Cownes

Cownes, the home of Major Beverly Browne Douglas, was built in 1857 of brick made on the place. The name was that of a former owner, A Scotchman-hence the pronunciation "Coons", as a cow to a Scotchman is always a "coo". When Major Douglas bought the place, there was a frame building, the overseer's house, surrounded by a grove of locust trees. This was afterwards used as the kitchen. Before building, Major Douglas had many forest trees set out, some of which, notably a swamp white oak, excite the admiration of all who see them. Many of the old locusts are still standing, though many have been blown down by storms. The place is occupied by two of Major Douglas' daughters (Mrs. Moncure and Mrs. Weathers) and in summer is the gathering place of his grandchildren and great-grandchildren.

Brighton

This is one of the oldest houses in the county, but we have no record of who built it, or who originally owned it. About the year 1846 it was bought, with Cownes, from a Mr. Broaddus of Caroline County by Major Beverly Browne Douglas of New Kent County and his wife, Eliza Dandridge, a daughter of Robert Pollard, Jr. of "Zoar". After the birth of their daughter, Bessie, they sold Brighton and lived at Zoar while a brick building was being put up at Cownes. Brighton has been owned by a number of different people since that time. It has recently been bought by Mrs. Howard L. Clarke of Newport, Rhode Island, and she has beautifully restored the old house and is much interested in improving the grounds and outbuildings.[11]

Figure 22. The main house at Brighton in the 1940s. (Source: The William and Mary Quarterly and Elizabeth H. Ryland in King William County, Virginia from Old Newspapers & Files, 1955)

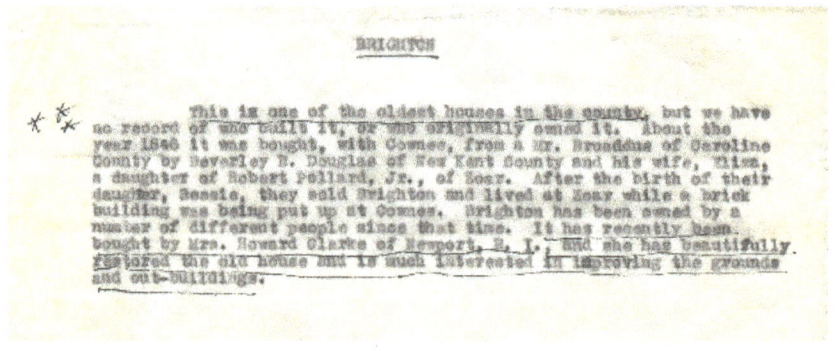

Figure 23. Description of Brighton and nearby local farms by Elizabeth Hawes Ryland (date unknown). (Source: Kelly family archive)

Figure 24. Barn and outbuildings at Brighton in the 1950s. (Source: Kelly family archive)

The early occupants of plantation homes such as these were generally well off. Families who were descendants of English gentry created impressive buildings and landscapes reminiscent of their homeland across the sea.

> In these old mansions a former generation lived in lordly manner and entertained with lavish hospitality...Time was when King William's homes resounded with mirth and pleasure, and her noble sons and stately daughters spent their time in routs and balls, and the old rafters of the ancient buildings echoed to the music and graceful steps of the minuet. The visits and goings about, the big dinners and parties, fish-fries and frolics occupied their time to the exclusion of most other matters, and it is no wonder the old churches fell into decay. The parson, however, was not entirely disregarded. His services were in demand for weddings, christenings, and burials, all of which functions were made the occasion of much ceremony and feasting. A certain gentleman from North Carolina having wooed and won a charming young lady of King William, who figures in this record, came on to claim his bride and many times have I heard the account of his arrival with his great yellow coach and six

splendid black horses, with grooms and footmen in livery, and half a dozen friends as outriders; his elegant apparel and courtly manners, the magnificent jewels and presents for the bridesmaids and attendants. How a whole month was consumed in "one continual round of pleasure" ere they bade farewell and started on the return to his Carolina home.[12]

Further verification of Brighton's early years as a modest plantation home, cited in the 2014 Architectural Survey of King William, lists 1765 as the original construction date of the house, rather than the date of 1750 noted on the 2014 county assessment documents. The surveyors described the plantations that became established in the early years of that era.

By the mid-eighteenth century, throughout the Tidewater prime agricultural land had been settled. What land remained generally was of poor quality. Newly constructed plantation and larger dwellings during the second half of the eighteenth century included "Belleview", "Brighton", "The Grove", and "Marle Hill", among others, and reflected the prosperity that the alluvial floodplains had bequeathed to planters. The emergence of the Georgian ideal of the plantation had arrived. The great planters surrounded their manor homes with associated dependencies and formal and utilitarian gardens. Beyond the core of the plantation lay numerous outbuildings and quarters. Outlying farms were typically home to a group of enslaved laborers and perhaps an overseer. Roads had an irregular quality in response to the influence of the region's great planters.[13]

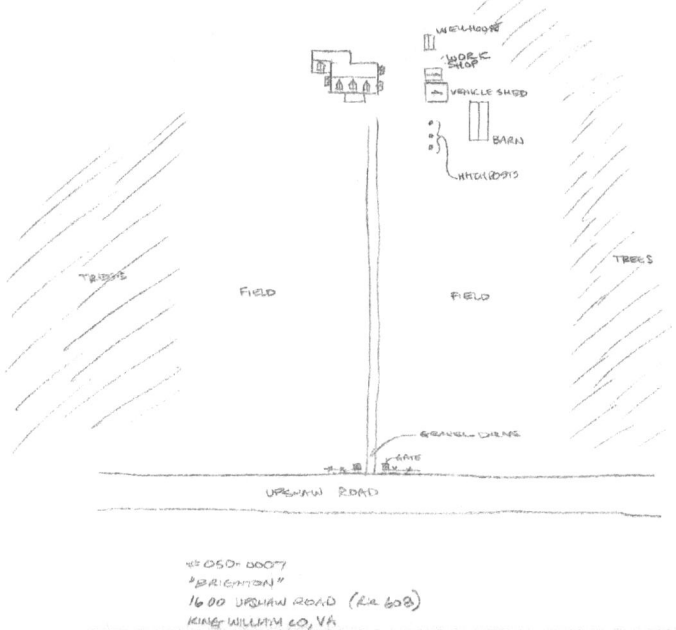

Figure 25. Sketch of Brighton property in an Architectural Survey in 2014 showing the location of the house, barn, outbuildings and hitching posts. (Source: Stantec 2014)

Figure 26. Grape arbor and sundial in the backyard at Brighton in the early 1950s. (Source: Kelly family archive)

While the original builder/owner of Brighton remains a mystery, the construction date of "circa 1750" appears consistent with the distinctive architectural style of that time. The original house, built in three multilevel sections to reduce local tax liability, comprised one "room," defined as a basement, first story, and upper half story. By building one section at a time, in the early "hall and parlor" plan, the owner paid taxes on only one or more "rooms" or sections.[14] This architectural style, influenced by the Palladian and Georgian styles, evolved between 1700 and 1860 and focused on creating symmetry by walling off the corridor to create the "center-passage" house. The style, which was quite common in Virginia and Maryland, was also known as the center-hall house, the hall-passage-parlor house, the Williamsburg cottage, and the Tidewater-type house.[15]

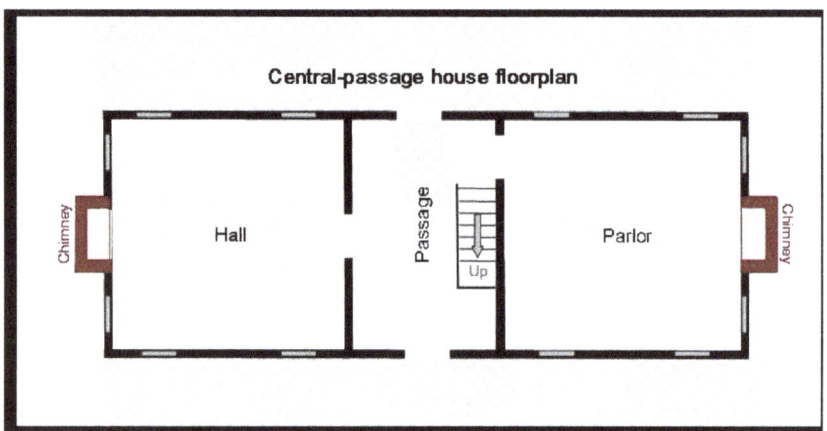

Figure 27. Central passage-house floor plan illustrating the hall and parlor plan with symmetrical chimneys as was common in the 18th century in Virginia and Maryland. (Source: Wikipedia Commons)

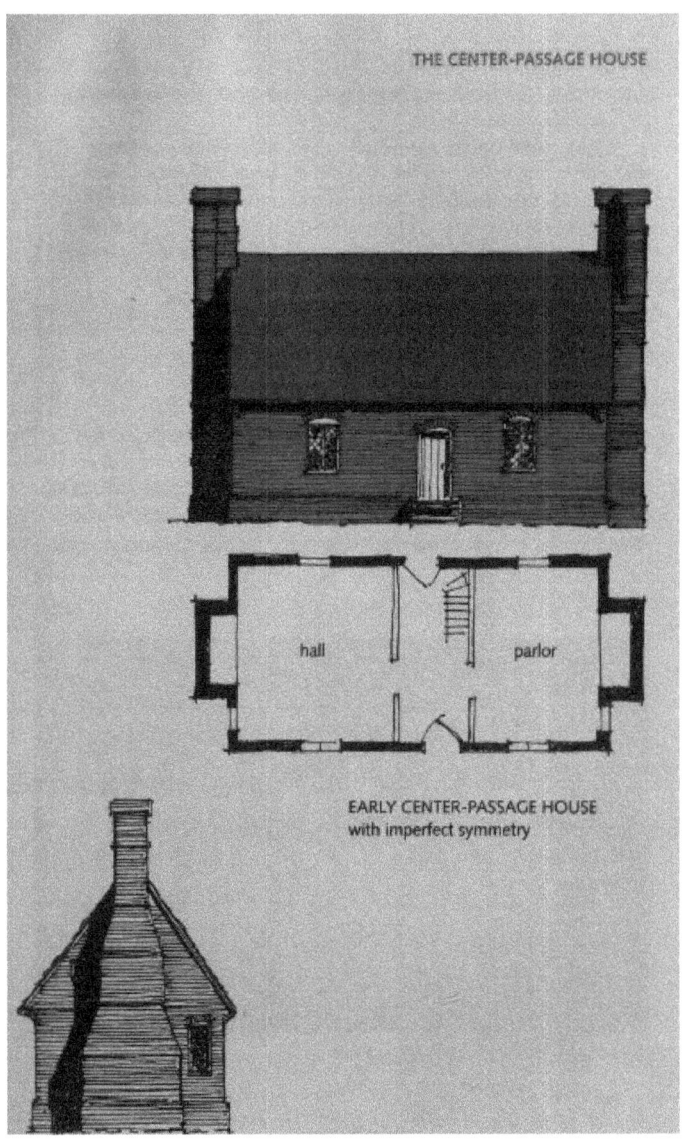

Figure 28. The Center-passage house illustrating the typical floor plan of early Virginia homes. (Source: Gerald Foster)

Figure 29. *The original center hall and parlor floor plan has been maintained at Brighton since the house was constructed in 1750. (Source: The Steele Group Sotheby's International Realty)*

In the original building, Brighton was one-and-a-half stories and one room deep. The builders constructed the house on a raised brick foundation with large-stepped brick chimneys on either end. A stair to the steep-roofed second story, built in the center passage with wide doorways at the front and rear, allowed for drafts to cool the upper level in the hot and humid summer months. Dormer windows allowed light and airflow into the upper rooms. Over the centuries, the house at Brighton has maintained this original form, with various upgrades and additions to the basement (for example, moving the original kitchen, which was housed in a separate building nearby, into the basement of the main house) and to the front and rear of the house (porches, sunroom, extra fireplaces, a dining room, and an attached two car garage). Even though owners made renovations to much of the original construction over the centuries, a view through some of the main floor windows today reveals imperfections and small bubbles in hand-blown glass, likely created centuries earlier.

Figure 30. The house at Brighton contains two dormer bedrooms on the second floor. (Source: The Steele Group Sotheby's International Realty)

Figure 31. The house at Brighton has brick chimneys of similar style that have been maintained since the mid-eighteenth century. (Source: Kelly family archive)

Figure 32. Polished pine floors, bookcases with glass doors and handblown glass in the windows were traditional features in the house at Brighton. (Source: The Steele Group Sotheby's International Realty)

Elizabeth Ryland's research in 1935 further revealed that the acreage or tracts of land comprising Brighton and adjacent properties were owned by various members of the Hill families and/or their estates in King William County, Virginia. It's proved challenging to discern absolute ownership of overlapping acreages during those early years. The proposed chronology in the next chapter is the most probable timeline of the various families that owned, farmed, and/or lived at Brighton. Documents denoting state and county taxes, based on varying tract sizes, support this chronology.

It's interesting to note in these records that acreages and tracts of land were often approximated, with notations of "more or less" in the sales transactions, even as they moved between and within families. Besides land taxes, the government taxed landowners on buildings and personal property that included slaves, horses, and cattle. In 1782, presumed Brighton landowner and widow Jemima (or Jermima) Tignor was taxed on 140 acres of land and two slaves, three horses, and seven cattle. The adjacent larger estate of the Hill family was taxed on almost 1,500 acres as well as forty-nine slaves, fifteen horses, and fifty-six cattle. These two families owned or occupied most of the properties located approximately twelve to thirteen miles northwest of the King William Courthouse, which would include the current property of Brighton.[16] Personal property tax records verified that in 1820 Elizabeth Tignor and her husband John Burch, a shop owner in Aylett, owned 125 acres that included Brighton. Robert B. Hill and his brother John Hill, Jr. owned the surrounding acreage, which they inherited from their father, Colonel Humphrey Hill. The next chapter provides details about the property encompassing Brighton, which remained within the Hill family well into the nineteenth century.[17]

1. Nugent, Nell Marion. *Cavaliers and Pioneers: Abstracts of Virginia Land Patents and Grants, 1623–1782.* 8 vols and supplement (vols. 4–8 published by the Virginia Genealogical Society, Dennis Hudgins ed.) (Ref. F225 N841)
2. Colonial Land Office Patents, 1623–1774. Library of Virginia. https://www.lva.virginia.gov/public/guides/opac/lonnabout.htm
3. King William County Land Office Records. Virginia State Archives. Book 9, 554, as cited in Personal communication to Mrs. Clark from Elizabeth Ryland, 1935.
4. *Virginia Quit Rent Rolls, 1704.* The Virginia Magazine of History and Biography, Jul. 1920, Vol. 28, No. 3 (Jul. 1920), 207–218. Published by Virginia Historical Society Stable URL: https://www.jstor.org/stable/4243771
5. Hysing, Hans. Virginia Historical Society, Public Domain. https://commons.wikimedia.org/w/index.php?curid=4620238
6. Ruffin, Edmund, (Ed.) (1841). Byrd, William (author) *The Westover Manuscripts: Containing the History of the Dividing Line Betwixt Virginia and North Carolina; A Journey to the Land of Eden,* A. D. 1733; and *A Progress to the Mines.* Written from 1728 to 1736. Petersburg: Edmund and Julian, Pub.
7. Byrd, William. "*A Progress to the Mines in the Year 1732* (142–143), published as part of "*The Westover Manuscripts*" in 1841. https://docsouth.unc.edu/nc/byrd/menu.html
8. *The Hill Family of Virginia,* compiled by Mrs. Giles C. Courtney, nee Elizabeth Spotswood Hill, 1905.
9. Fleet, Beverly. (1988) *Virginia Colonial Abstracts,* 343. Baltimore: Clearfield Company, Inc.
10. Grymes, Charles A. "Acquiring Virginia Land by Headright." virginiaplaces.org
11. Personal Communication (1935): Ryland letter to Mrs. Clark describing KW homes and properties, including Brighton.
12. Clarke, Patricia Neale. (1897) *Old King William Homes and families: An account of some of the old homesteads and families of King William County, Virginia, from its earliest settlement,*

7. Louisville, J. P. Morton and Co. https://archive.org/details/oldkingwilliamho00clar/page/6/mode/2up
13. Upton, Dell. (1988) New Views of the Virginia Landscape. *The Virginia Magazine of History and Biography* 96, no.4: 403–47 as cited in *An Architectural Survey of King William County (Cost Share 2014)* Stantec Consulting Services, Formerly CRI (July 24, 2014), 5.22.
14. "Central-passage house," *Wikipedia, The Free Encyclopedia*, https://en.wikipedia.org/w/index.php?title=Central-passage_house&oldid=1008364250 (accessed March 23, 2021).
15. Foster, Gerald. (2004) *American Houses*. 94–95. Houghton Mifflin. https://archive.org/details/americanhousesfi00fost/page/94/mode/2up
16. Ward, Roger. (1998) *1815 Directory of Virginia Landowners*. Vol. 3 eastern Region. Iberian Pub. Co: Athens, GA.
17. Weaver, Jeffrey. (1998) *1782 King William County, Virginia Personal Property Tax List*. Government Tax Files. New River Notes. https://www.newrivernotes.com/neighboring_kingwilliam_enumerations_1782_personalpropertytax.htm

CHAPTER III
Chronology of "Brighton" Owners 1786–1854

Figure 33. Guests enjoying the breeze on the front porch at Brighton. (Source: Kelly family archive)

> "Many of my friends in King William County were descendants of prominent early families in Virginia. It was not uncommon for families to maintain properties over the centuries and to proudly share stories of their ancestors, particularly those who were patriots in the struggle for Virginia's independence."

As mentioned previously, the style and content of the information recorded in Virginia's personal property tax records fluctuated over the years. In 2011, a Library of Virginia archivist, Minor T. Weisiger, offered an explanation in his research notes.

> *Information recorded in Virginia personal property tax records changed gradually from 1782 to 1865. The early laws required the tax commissioner in each district to record in "a fair alphabetical list" the names of the person chargeable with the tax, the names of white male tithables over the age of twenty-one, the number of white male tithables between ages sixteen and twenty-one, the number of slaves both above and below age sixteen, various types of animals such as horses and cattle, carriage wheels, ordinary licenses, and even billiard tables.[1]*

According to the King William County substitute census list, in 1810, there were "766 households, 760 tithables (individuals required to pay taxes), both white and free black, and 3,070 slaves over the age of twelve, and 1,793 horses."[2] In 1813, the land tax records noted the nearest landmarks (creek, river, road, etc.), and by 1815, these records included the location of properties in relation to distance from the county courthouse.[3]

While the King William County Courthouse is approximately twelve to thirteen miles from Brighton, the closest town to the property was, and still is, Aylett (or Ayletts), about three miles away. Aylett occupies land granted to William Aylett in 1685 by King Charles II of England, who was credited with nicknaming Virginia "The Old Dominion." Before 1861 and the start of the Civil War, the population of Aylett consisted of 250 individuals who owned homes and businesses clustered near the southeast bank of the Mattaponi River. Several tobacco warehouses were in operation, and this section of the river served as an important transportation hub for the region before, during, and after the war years.

> *Before the War Between the States the town bristled with activity each Tuesday and Friday, when people of the countryside drove in to meet the stage, which brought the "United States mail"—including newspapers. The lumbering stage, drawn by four horses, ran between Tappahannock and Richmond; on its "boot" were trunks, and on its top packages and mail bags. "Mail days" were shopping days and people brought their lunches with them. In 1856 Ayletts had a carriage factory, an iron foundry, tailoring and millinery shops, a tavern, harness and saddlemaking plants, and a variety of stores.[4]*

One of those stores, Burch and Sweets Dry Goods, was co-owned by John Burch (husband of Elizabeth Tignor), who was listed in the King William tax records as an owner of Brighton between 1820 and 1830. Burch was again documented as a shop owner in Aylett in Elliott and Nye's 1852 *Virginia Directory and Business Register*, which stated that in King William County, "*The lands in this county are generally good; those on and near the rivers very fertile. Average value of the land by the assessment of 1850 $8.10 per acre. Population=8,793: whites 2,712, free colored 345, slaves 5,737. Number of persons over the age of 20 years who cannot read and write 204.*"[5]

Prior to and during Burch's ownership of acreage at Brighton, Ryland surmised that the Hill and Tigner/Tignor families owned most of the property, even as she stated in her 1935 review of old tax records, "*There is practically nothing earlier than 1813 to show the location of any King William lands in these old tax lists.*" However, based on her knowledge of the location of Brighton in relation to the Herring Creeks and the distance and direction from the King William Courthouse (twelve to thirteen miles NW), she verified that a portion of land comprising Brighton belonged to the Tignors, a family of chair makers (also recorded as Tigner in some documents), as she noted:

> In Book 2, p. 56, I found this deed: Dated 19 October 1786. Thomas Tignor and Elizabeth, his wife of St. David's Parish, sell to James Tignor a tract of land lying on the south side of the branch that leads from Herring Creek below Hill's Mill to the headspring near the said Thomas Tignor's house, which tract contained 17 and one-half acres. The deed is witnessed by John Hill, Thomas Elliott and James Elliott.

She also noted in the margin: "*Hill's Mill is believed to be the present Sizer's Mill.*"[6] A map of the area, drawn in 1863 for use by the Confederate troops, reveals that Sizer's Mill lies about two miles northeast of Brighton.[7]

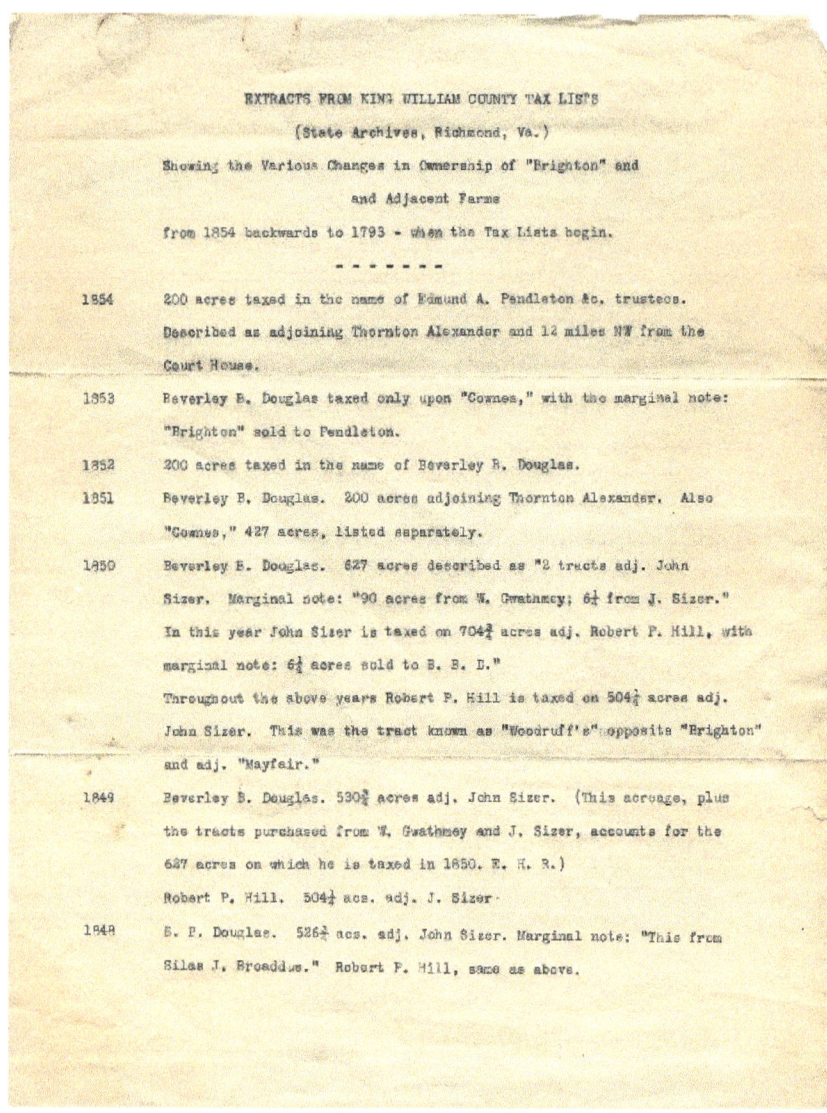

Figure 34. Extracts from King William County Tax Lists complied by Elizabeth Hawes Ryland for Mrs. Howard L. Clark in 1935. This document lists the various changes in ownership of Brighton and adjacent farms from 1793 to 1854. (Source: Kelly family archive)

As Ryland stated in her document on the history of Brighton, the following chronology of owners illustrates that during the pre–Civil War years of 1793–1854, various members of the Tignor (Tigner), Hill,

Burch, Broaddus, Douglas, and Pendleton families paid the land and property taxes. The full names of husbands, wives, various relatives, and neighbors are listed as completely as possible in the event that a reader might opt to pursue further verification. According to the author's recent attempts to verify land transactions, each entry below represents ownership of land that comprised part or all of the current Brighton property during this period.

Tignor/Tigner

1793 Jemima (Jermima) Tigner (a widow, deceased husband Curtis) taxed on 140 acres, in addition to two slaves, three horses, and seven cattle.

1810 Jemima Tigner sold fifteen acres and was taxed on 125 acres located adjacent to John Hill, Jr. and Robert Alexander (a neighboring landowner to Brighton as illustrated on the 1865 Civil War map[8]).

1813 Jemima Tigner taxed on 125 acres adjacent to John Hill, Jr. and Robert Alexander.

1816 William Tigner (son of Jemima) taxed on one hundred acres adjacent to John Hill, Jr. and Robert Alexander. Elizabeth Tigner (daughter of Jemima) taxed on twenty-five acres inherited from Jemima Tigner, adjacent to William Tigner.

1819 Elizabeth Tigner taxed on 125 acres after receiving one hundred acres from William Tigner, as per her mother's will (Jemima Tigner), following documented litigation/arbitration in the King William courts.[9]

1820 Elizabeth Tigner married John Burch, who takes ownership of her 125 acres by marriage (by law, married women turned over all property to their husbands). Burch was a hotel keeper and co-owner of *Burch and Sweets Dry Goods* in Aylett.

1826 John Burch taxed on 125 acres adjacent to John Hill, Jr. and Robert Alexander and 68.75 acres purchased from Robert Pollard, Jr. of Zoar.

1828 John Burch taxed on 193.75 acres adjacent to John Hill, Jr. and William Gatewood (a neighboring landowner).

1829 John Burch taxed on 106.5 acres after selling 83.25 acres to Edward Hill and 3.75 acres to Mary and Martha Gaines (wife of Robert B. Hill) and an extra $200 tax for buildings on property adjacent to John Hill, Jr. and William Gatewood.

Hill

In 1782, the Hill family, and in particular John Hill, the son of Colonel Humphrey Hill, owned over three thousand acres in King William county. During the American Revolution, his younger brother, Baylor, often visited John "*to engage in foxhunting and other sports and amusements that the area afforded.*" After John Hill's death in 1797, the executor of his estate divided the acreage among his seven children, including his sons, Robert B. Hill (of Woodroofe), John Hill, Jr., and Edward Hill, who "*enjoyed the life of the plantations, dancing, visiting, and hunting. It was an intriguing rural society.*"[10]

1810 Robert B. Hill and John Hill Jr. taxed on 997 and 500 acres. Together, they owned forty-nine slaves, fifteen horses, and fifty-six cattle.

1813 Robert B. Hill (estate) and John Hill, Jr. taxed on adjacent properties of 761 and 500 acres. During the previous years, Robert B. Hill, or his estate, sold 236 acres.

1816 Robert B. Hill (estate) taxed on 611 acres adjacent to John Hill, Jr. and John H. Walker after selling 150 acres to John and Baylor Hill, who, in 1818, traded under the firm name of John and Baylor Hill, Merchants and Partners. This transaction included Hill's Mill, later known as Sizer's Mill. John Hill, Jr. taxed on 582 acres on Herring Creek adjacent to Robert Hill's estate. (It's not clear when Hill acquired the extra eighty-two acres).

1831 Edward Hill taxed on 190 acres comprising two tracts: 83.25 acres purchased from John Burch, adjacent to John Hill, Jr., and 106.75 acres purchased from Robert B. Hill's estate.

John Hill, Jr. (estate) taxed on 562 acres on Herring Creek adjacent to Robert Hill's estate taxed on 611 acres, which became the Augustus Sizer property in 1840.

In her review of King William Land Records, Ryland described these transactions:

> "Subtract from this 611 acres the 106.75 acres by deed to Edward Hill, and we have the 504.25 shown as "Woodruff's" tract throughout the subsequent years."

Ryland also believed that:

> "Edward Hill's property consisted of two tracts: one of 106.75 acres, formerly of Robert Hill's estate and one of 83.25 acres adjoining John Hill's estate, later the Sizer property. The question is: which was Brighton? In either case, Brighton was for many years part of the Hill estates in King William Co."[11]

1834 Edward Hill taxed on 527.75 acres comprising three tracts: the original 190 acres (as above) plus 287.75 acres purchased from Phillip Aylett's estate Cownes (which comprised 550 acres on Herring Creek adjacent to Robert T. Gwathmey) and 49.5 acres purchased from Nathaniel B. Hill.

1839 Edward Hill taxed on 527.75 acres merged into two tracts: a plantation known as Cownes on the Mattaponi River and one property adjacent to the estate of John Hill, Jr., listed as Brighton. Robert Hill's estate was taxed on 504.25 acres adjacent to John Hill's estate and John H. Walker. John Hill's estate was taxed on 562 acres on Herring Creek and adjacent Robert Hill's estate (purchased the next year 1840 by John Sizer).

1840 Edward Hill taxed on 653 acres adjacent to Walker Hawes and Benjamin H. Mundy after purchasing 125.25 acres from Richard Gwathmey. Balance of Gwathmey's land sold to Silas J. Broaddus. Silas J. Broaddus taxed on 526.75 acres in two tracts, one on Mattaponi and one adjacent to John Sizer. (Edward Hill sold Cownes plantation and additional acres of Brighton to Silas Broaddus.)

Silas Broaddus, a "very ardent and zealous Methodist minister,"[12] was descended from Edward Broaddus, who was from Wales. His son and Silas's father, Thomas, also a minister, and many family members resided in nearby Caroline County. It is not known if Silas J. Broaddus ever lived at Brighton, or farmed the fields there, or rented the land to local farmers, as the two major occupations for the Broaddus family members were farmers and ministers.

Figure 35. Recovered abstract of land deed signed by Silas and Martha Broaddus for transactions with Beverly Browne Douglas, September 28, 1847. (Source: Burned Records, KWCHS)

1846 Silas J. Broaddus taxed on 526.75 acres comprising two tracts: Cownes Plantation and one property adjacent to John Sizer, purchased from Edward Hill, known as Brighton.

1848 Major Beverley Browne Douglas and his wife Eliza Dandridge Pollard of Zoar taxed on 526.75 acres consisting of the Cownes property and Brighton (189.75 acres), both having been purchased from Silas and Martha Broaddus on September 28, 1847.[13]

Much has been written about Major Beverley Browne Douglas (1822–1878), and a portrait of him hangs in the King William County Courthouse above the fireplace in the judge's chambers, along with other patriots who served King William County in a variety of official roles. Douglas was the son of William, who immigrated from Scotland and settled his family in New Kent County, Virginia. From 1839 to 1840, he attended the College of William and Mary and then decided to study medicine at the University of Edinburg while living with relatives in Scotland. Yet, after one session of agriculture, chemistry, and civil law in Scotland, he returned to Virginia to receive his law degree from William and Mary and eventually set up his law practice in Aylett in 1846. In 1847, he married Eliza Dandridge Pollard of Zoar (b. 1822), and they purchased Brighton, which they owned for several years. Douglas and Eliza lived at the farm for a time as newlyweds, a few miles from her family home. Their eldest daughter, Elizabeth Dandridge Douglas, or "Bessie," was born at Brighton on January 7, 1849.[14] Douglas also purchased the property known as Cownes (pronounced "Coons" after the Scottish word "coo" which refers to Highland cows), on the Mattaponi River, next to his father-in-law's property at Zoar; however, it was not until 1857 that he built the brick mansion which still stands today. Before moving to Cownes and after the birth of their daughter Bessie, they lived at Zoar. Zoar was actually named Mt. Zoar, as it stood on a hill overlooking the town of Aylett, which was considered a "modern Sodom and Gomorrah" and the "*wickedest place of its size in this part of the world.*"[15] Throughout these years, Douglas became engaged in Virginia politics and was outspoken on a range of issues that led to the American Civil War.

Figure 36. Portrait of Major Beverley Browne Douglas (1822-1878) (Source: Library of Congress. https://www.loc.gov/pictures/item/2017894605/)

1849 Beverley Browne Douglas taxed on 530.75 acres, including tracts purchased from William Gwathmey and John Sizer.

1850 Beverley Browne Douglas taxed on 627 acres comprising two tracts adjacent to John Sizer, including ninety acres purchased from William Gwathmey and 6.25 acres purchased from John Sizer.

1851 Beverley Browne Douglas taxed on two hundred acres, known as Brighton, adjacent to Thomas Alexander and 427 acres of Cownes plantation, where he and Eliza built a brick home in 1857.

Douglas was a member of the Virginia Constitutional Convention of 1850–51 and served in the Virginia State Senate from 1852 to 1865, representing King William, King and Queen, and Essex Counties. In June 1861, Douglas was commissioned into the Confederate States Army as a first lieutenant in Company H of the 9th Regiment of the Virginia Calvary. Company H was also known as "Lee's Rangers" as it was organized by Captain William Henry Fitzhugh ("Rooney") Lee, the second eldest son of General Robert E. Lee. During the war, the rangers composed the Sharpshooting Squadron and took part in fifty-three battles and skirmishes. As the war progressed and Rooney Lee rose to the status of colonel, Douglas was promoted to captain in Company H and in 1862 to major in the 5th Virginia Calvary before resigning from military service in 1863 to focus on his political career.[16,17]

In 1851, a decade before the war began, Douglas sold two hundred acres "of a place called Brighton" to Edmund A. Pendleton's estate, and more specifically to his heirs, Edmund S. Pendleton and Patrick Henry Pendleton.[18] Major Douglas moved from Brighton to Zoar, his wife Eliza Pollard's home, once it was rebuilt, following a fire rumored to have been set by a servant in 1851. Reportedly, she wanted the family to move to Richmond so that she could be near her boyfriend.

Figure 37. Recovered abstract of land transaction between Douglas and Edmund and Patrick Henry Pendleton for a 'certain tract or parcel of land in King William on the south side of the main road leading from Aylett to Mangohick containing by estimation two hundred acres of a place called Brighton,' 1851. (Source: Burned Records KWCHS)

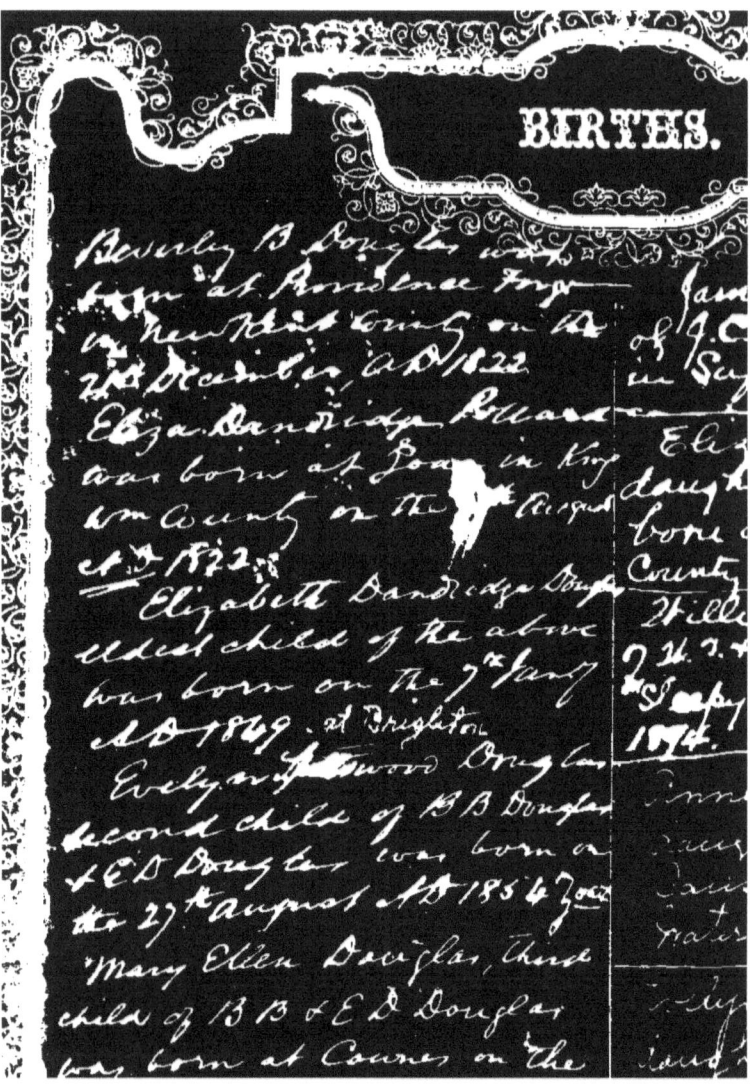

Figure 38. Birth records in the Douglas Family Bible noting that Beverley Douglas was born December 21, 1822 in Providence Forge, New Kent County. His wife, Elizabeth Dandridge Pollard was born at Zoar in King William County in August 1822. Their eldest child, Elizabeth "Bessie" Dandridge Douglas was born at Brighton on January 7, 1849. (Source: Douglas Family Bible, Library of Virginia. http://image.lva. virginia.gov/Bible/32870/index.html?_ga=2.224531226.141364856.1616 536019-922006287.1607813578)

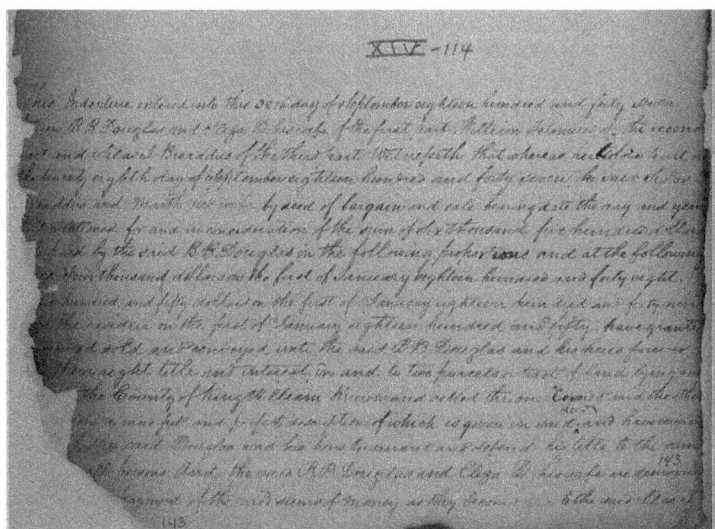

Figure 39. Recovered record dated September 28, 1847 detailing the Douglas's purchase of Cownes plantation from Silas Broaddus. (Source: Burned records, KWCHS)

Following the war, Douglas continued to engage in the political arena and was elected to the US House of Representatives in 1874 and re-elected in 1876, serving until his death in 1878. Throughout his tenure in politics, it was well known that he "*drank alcohol in excess, which may have fueled his hair-trigger temper.*" During a debate for the 1874 seat, he responded to an accusation of lying from his Republican opponent, James Beverley Sener, by hurling a glass tumbler at him, which resulted in further heated exchanges and a broken arm and nose for incumbent Sener. There are also stories of friends having to intervene and negotiate settlements to avoid duels that were often precipitated by harsh newspaper editorials and public insults, including one such altercation with another Virginia congressional representative just days before Douglas's death in a Washington, DC, hotel. His final resting place is at his wife's family home Zoar near Aylett, where his gravestone reads, "*He was an honest politician.*"[19,20]

In 1854, the Edmund A. Pendleton estate was taxed on two hundred acres known as Brighton adjacent to Thomas Alexander and twelve miles from the King William Courthouse. The estate of Judge Edmund

A. Pendleton (1788–1803) of Caroline County was complex as he had no living heirs. His nephew of the same name inherited most of his property. Also a judge, Edmund Pendleton, Jr. (to differentiate him from his uncle) lived at his uncle's plantation "Edmundton" in Caroline County, and the family estate included many farms in the area.[21,22]

When Douglas and his wife sold Brighton, the land deed noted that Edmund S. Pendleton and Patrick Henry Pendleton and their heirs would have rights to Brighton, which included two hundred acres south of the main road leading from Aylett to Mangohick. The land deed further noted that Douglas might have sold two other tracts of land, one to "J. Dandridge (his wife or a relative?) and another to Billy Gordon. The documentation is challenging to decipher as these land deeds are part of the thousands of recovered burned records detailing land transactions from 1702 to 1884. This may have been one of the last transactions of the Brighton property prior to the American Civil War (April 1861–May 1865). On June 10, 1861, Brighton was recorded as the home of Captain Thomas Witt Haynes; however, land transaction documents have not been located that would support his purchase of the property. Haynes joined Beverley Browne Douglas and William "Rooney" Lee to lead Company H and Lee's Rangers in the War Between the States or, for some southerners, "The War of Northern Aggression."[23]

Figure 40. Original brick pumphouse at Brighton. During the summer months this building served as a cool place to store perishable food such as ice and, in later years, ice cream. (Source: Kelly family archive)

Figure 41. Road bordering the fields behind Brighton with fences for livestock. (Source: Kelly family archive)

1. Vogt, John. (2011) *King William County, VA 1810 Substitute Census* [Abstracts from the 1810 Personal Property Tax List] https://heritagebooks.com/products/king-william-county-va-1810-substitute-census
2. King William County, Virginia https://genealogyresources.org/King_William.html
3. Ward, Roger. (1998) *1815 Directory of Virginia Landowners. Vol. 3 Eastern Region.* Iberian Pub. Co: Athens, GA.
4. *Virginia Guide to the Old Dominion.* (1992) Compiled by Workers of the Writers' Program of the Work Projects Administration in the State of Virginia. Virginia State Library and Archives. Tour 20 http://xroads.virginia.edu/~Hyper/VAGuide/TOUR20.html
5. *Elliott and Nye's Virginia Directory and Business Register.* (1852) King William County, New River Notes. Historical and Genealogical Resources for the Upper River Valley of North Carolina and Virginia. https://www.newrivernotes.com/topical_business_1852_elliott_nye_directory.htm#
6. Ryland, Elizabeth. (1935) Personal Communication. "History of Brighton According to Land Records. Presented to Mrs. Howard L. Clark, owner of Brighton."
7. Hotchkiss, J., Grant, J., Barrows, A. S., et al. (1863) *Map of King William County, Va.* [Map] Retrieved from the Library of Congress, http://hdl.loc.gov/loc.gmd/g3883k.cwh00042
8. Confederate States of America. Army. Dept. of Northern Virginia. Chief Engineer's Office and Blackford, B. L. (1865) *Map of King William County, VA* [S.l.: Chief Engineer's Office, D.N.V] [Map] Retrieved from the Library of Congress. https://www.loc.gov/item/gvhs01.vhs00351/.
9. King William County Virginia Records Land Transactions, Burned Records Files 1702–1884. Book 8, 27–28, King William County Historical Society.
10. Harris, Malcolm H. (1977) *Old New Kent County [Virginia] Some account of the planters, plantations and places.* Vol II, 845. King William County, West Point, VA.

11. Ryland, Elizabeth. (1935) Personal Communication. "History of Brighton According to Land Records. Presented to Mrs. Howard L. Clark, owner of Brighton."
12. Broaddus, Andrew. (1888) A *History of the Broaddus Family: from the time of the settlement of the progenitor of the family in the United States down to the year 1888*, 41. https://archive.org/details/historyofbroaddu00broa/page/40/mode/2up
13. King William County Virginia Records Land Transactions, Burned Records Files 1702–1884. Book 13, 141–144, King William County Historical Society.
14. Douglas family Bible records. Library of Virginia http://image.lva.virginia.gov/Bible/32870/index.html?_ga=2.112238084.1873765329.1606066455-731966405.1598729338
15. Harris, Malcolm H. (1977) *Old New Kent County [Virginia] Some account of the planters, plantations and places*. Vol II, 839. King William County. West Point, VA.
16. Atkinson, Dorothy. (1990) *King William County in the Civil War, Along Mangohick Byways*. Heritage Books, Inc. MD.
17. Beverly B. Douglas https://en.wikipedia.org/wiki/Beverly_B._Douglas; "Q851699," *Wikidata*, https://www.wikidata.org/w/index.php?title=Q851699&oldid=1293141701 (accessed March 24, 2021)
18. King William County Virginia Records Land Transactions, Burned Records Files 1702–1884. Book 14, 275. King William County Historical Society.
19. The Bulletin of the King William County Historical Society (October 1979, no. 6). *Lee's Rangers*.
20. Sara B. Bearss. "Beverley Browne Douglas (1822–1878)," *Dictionary of Virginia Biography*, Library of Virginia (1998–) published 2016. http://www.lva.virginia.gov/public/dvb/bio.asp?b=Douglas_Beverley_Brown
21. Page, Richard. (1883) Genealogy of the Page Family in Virginia: Also a Condensed Account of the Nelson, Walker, Pendleton, and Randolph Families. New York: Jenkins and Thomas, Printers.

https://archive.org/details/genealogypagefa00pagegoog/page/n224/mode/2u
22. Edmund Pendleton. https://en.wikipedia.org/wiki/Edmund_Pendleton
23. Atkinson, Dorothy. (1990) *King William County in the Civil War, Along Mangohick Byways.* 24. Heritage Books, Inc., MD.

CHAPTER IV
Brighton: The War Years, Reconstruction, and the 20th Century 1855 to 1952

"For many years, a large, framed print of Confederate generals was on display in the center hallway at Brighton. It seemed to speak to the southern perspective of 'The War of Northern Aggression'. As a teenager I acquired an intense fascination with the stories of Virginia's families amid the devastation and drama that ensued between the north and the south. My awareness of the civil and social issues that arose during the war years contributed to my engagement in similar issues today. "

LEE RANGERS
Co. H 9th Regt. Va. Cavalry

This Company was organized at West Point, King William County Virginia in June 1861, with the following commissioned officers:
  Captain Wm. H. F. Lee
  1st Lieut. Beverley B. Douglas
  2nd Lieut. James Pollard
From West Point the Company marched to camp of instruction for Cavalry (at Ashland, Hanover County Va.) where, after being drilled for several weeks by Colonels Field and Lomax, it was ordered to Northwestern Va. where it spent the winter of 1861-62: in the latter part of the winter of 1862, it was ordered to Fredericksburg where we were regularly drilled until The Campaign opened in the spring, when the 9th Regiment of Virginia Cavalry was organized with the following ten companies:
  Company A Stafford County Virginia
  Company B Caroline County Virginia
  Company C Westmoreland County Virginia
  Company D Lancaster County Virginia
  Company E Spotsylvania County Virginia
  Company F Essex County Virginia
  Company G Lunenburg County Virginia
  Company H (Lee Rangers Virginia and other States & Countries)
  Company I King George County Virginia
  Company K Richmond County Virginia
The following is the Roll of Company H. 9th Regt. Virginia Cavalry (Lee Rangers) from June 1861 to April 1865:
  Captains: Chas. A. Harrison
    Wm. H. F. Lee   Alfred Morrison
    B. B. Douglas   John Ells
    Thos. W. Haynes   John Pemberton

Figure 42. Lee's Rangers. (Source: KW County Historical Society newsletter)

As in the past decades, Brighton continued to change ownership. Before the start of the Civil War, an attorney, Thomas Witt Haynes (1827–1877), occupied the property. Educated at the University of Virginia, Haynes graduated as the valedictorian in 1850 and set up his law practice in Aylett soon after Beverley Browne Douglas. Both men served as King William County Commissioners.[1]

In April 1859, according to deeds recorded in the *King William County Burned Records*, Thomas Haynes and Brooking Samuel applied to the county for "*a license to keep a house of entertainment in Aylett*" for a fee of $200. The court was of "*the opinion that the applicant is sober and of good character, and will probably keep a house orderly, useful and such as the law requires.*" The court document further noted that the applicants needed to:

> "*...faithfully observe all laws regulating houses of entertainment, and all laws in relation to dealing with slaves, free negroes and selling ardent spirits, wine and any mixture thereof or any other intoxicating liquor to slaves as contained in Chapter one hundred and four of the Code of Virginia then the above obligation to be void, otherwise to remain in full force and virtue.*"[2]

A location or description of the house of entertainment had not been established at the time of this writing. Could it have been at Brighton?

On June 10, 1861, when Haynes enlisted as a sergeant in the Confederate States Army, he noted that the farm at Brighton was his home as documented by Dorothy Atkinson, in *King William County in the Civil War, Along Mangohick Byways*.[3] Over a century later, the Kelly children would discover Civil War buttons and bullets on the property. In her book, Atkinson describes in great detail the campaigns of the War Between the States and the movements of both armies throughout the county. In particular, she chronicles their marches along Route 30, "The King William Highway," and also along Route 608 past Brighton and Warsaw plantations, on their way to the Mattaponi River for transportation to West Point or Yorktown.[4]

She relates that soon after the war began, Haynes rode with Colonel William Aylett and thirty-five others from King William County to form the nucleus of Taylor's Grays, a calvary unit under Colonel Harrison B. Tomlin of West Point, Virginia. As units expanded and reformed during the war, the military promoted Haynes from sergeant to lieutenant and then to captain in William "Rooney" Lee's Rangers, the Sharpshooter Squadron of the 9th Virginia Cavalry, Company H.[5] In the early years of the war, Haynes helped to lead the company in many skirmishes and battles, along with B.B. Douglas and Rooney Lee.

He was wounded twice, first at the Battle of Upperville on June 21, 1863, and again at Manassas/Bristow Station on October 15, 1863. Even though he survived his wounds, he retired to the Invalid Corps on March 13, 1863, and lived for fourteen more years, all the while suffering from paralysis due to injuries to his spine. Before the war, he served as a county commissioner, and then after the war served as county treasurer, which is why his portrait hangs in the King William County Courthouse.[6]

Figure 43. Portrait of Captain Thomas Witt Haynes. (Source: David Kelly)

Prior to the war, Haynes married Mollie Hawes (1835–1860), sister of Walker Aylett Hawes, another sharpshooter who served in Company H.[7] Their home, designated as "Capt. Haynes" on Blackford's 1865 Civil War Map (see Figure 45), drawn by the Chief Engineer's Office, sits on the exact location of present-day Brighton.[8]

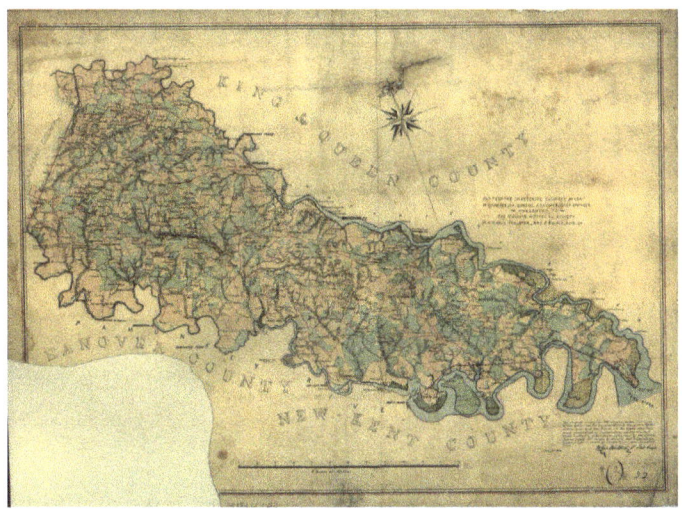

Figure 44. 1865 Civil War Engineer's map. (Source: Blackford, 1865)

Figure 45. Civil War map with Aylett and Haynes home at Brighton. (Source: Blackford, 1865)

A similar map (see Figure 46), dated 1863, shows the home of Captain Haynes at the end of a long lane leading south off from Upshaw Road. Neighbors included Dr. Robert Alexander to the south, Baylor Hill to the east, and Augustus and John Sizer to the northeast. Nearby properties and plantations of the Pollard family, which included Zoar, Warsaw, Octagon, and Edgehill, are also documented on the map.[9]

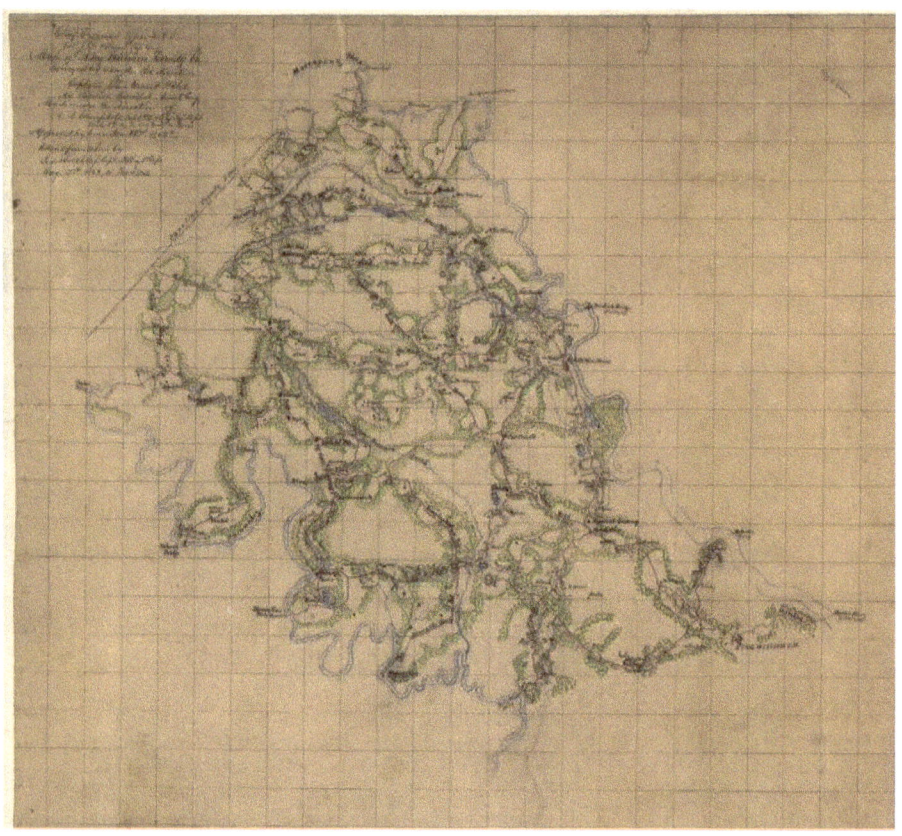

Figure 46. 1863 Map of King William County. (Source: Hotchkiss, et al 1863)

Haynes died in 1877, and his grave, along with Mollie and three of his young children, Martha, Lottie, and Emma, who all predeceased him, are in the cemetery at his wife's family home, The Grove plantation. His gravestone shows the great respect he had from his fellow Virginians.

> In Memory of Capt. Thomas Witt Haynes Born Aug 12, 1827, Died May 4, 1877. For more than thirteen years a helpless paralysed subject to almost incessant pain caused by a gunshot wound to the spine received in battle, he bore the severest bodily suffering with heroic fortitude: rendering himself under the greatest disadvantage eminently useful in important public relations which he filled. A brave soldier, a genial companion distinguished by almost every noble and generous quality, he allowed himself a host of friends who loved and admired him while living and mourn over his death.[10]

After returning home from the war, it is not clear how long Thomas Haynes lived at Brighton or if he and his family lived at The Grove to receive support for his extensive health needs. His father-in-law, Dr. Aylett Hawes, was a beloved family physician in King William County for many years. He purchased The Grove plantation (also known as Wormley Grove), which included 849 acres along the Pamunkey River, in 1840.

On November 7, 1903, a *Richmond-Times Dispatch* obituary for Haynes's son, also named Thomas Haynes and also a graduate of the University of Virginia, noted that the young Haynes resembled his father, who was "desperately wounded during the war" and "was never able to walk."[11] The elder Haynes moved about in a wheelchair, even to church, and one of his former slaves, "who was untiring in his devotion to his former master," attended to his needs. Haynes's wife, Mollie, died in 1860 at the young age of twenty-five, and Haynes's son, Thomas, sold Brighton. At the time of the sale in May 1888, the young Thomas Haynes lived in San Antonio, Texas.[12]

In 1888, reconstruction of the southern states was well underway, and economic change was taking shape in Virginia. West Point, the principal town in King William County, at the head of the York River, had a population of over 2200. West Point was the termination of the Richmond, York, and Chesapeake railroad. There were several large steamship lines from this point to New York, Boston, and Baltimore, and a weekly line to the head of navigation on the Mattaponi River, at Aylett. The water at the Aylett wharves was of sufficient depth to admit the largest class vessels, especially as nearby landowners dredged the river. Following the war, the average assessed value of land had decreased from pre-war years, when it sold for $8.10 an acre, to $6.60 per acre in 1888. During the emancipation years, landowners entered into labor contracts with former slaves, and a system of sharecropping emerged. Tobacco became Virginia's most lucrative cash crop, and steamships and railroads transported Virginia products across the country and around the world. In fact, restaurants served such delicacies as oysters harvested in the early morning from the Chesapeake Bay to patrons in New York restaurants later that same day. And, as education became a political agenda, it's interesting to note that King William County taxpayers, during the reconstruction years, supported nineteen white and nineteen other (Indian and African American) schools throughout the county.[13]

It was during 1888 that Thomas Haynes, the son of Captain Thomas Haynes, sold Brighton to Thomas N. Walker for approximately $2,000, with a dwelling, outbuildings, and land comprising three hundred acres ($6.67 per acre). The property description noted that the land was bounded by the public road leading from Aylett to Mangohick, Clement's Mill, the lands of Joe Hay, A. Tuck, and A. Sizer. The deed, recorded on March 25, 1889, makes no mention of his wife, Mollie ("marriage silent").[14]

Thomas Walker was a descendant of a Virginia physician, surveyor, and explorer, also named Thomas Walker, who had been born in King and Queen County near the present-day town of Walkerton. While historians note that the elder Dr. Walker (1715–1794) was a notable figure in the Virginia patriot's league as he corresponded with the likes of Thomas Jefferson, George Washington, and James Madison, the great-grandson Walker was not as well known. Dr. Thomas Walker, the father of twelve children, is also known for his extensive surveys of Virginia's state boundaries and assisted with establishing state borders, or "the Walker Line" between Virginia, North Carolina, Kentucky, and Tennessee.[15,16]

Two years later, Walker and his wife sold Brighton on July 1, 1890, and they transferred the property of three hundred acres to James W. Kidd and his wife, who owned Brighton for seven years.[17] On May 24, 1897, Roy Taylor purchased Brighton from J. W. Kidd. Records from the Land Deeds Books showed that Taylor and his wife, Annie, maintained ownership for over two decades when ownership transferred once again, within the Taylor family, on March 31, 1919.[18]

There is no explanation in the county land records as to why Roy and Annie Taylor transferred the deed for Brighton to (sons? relatives?) Hiram P. Taylor and Holcolme (Holcombe) W. Taylor on March 31, 1919. What followed was a sequence of transactions involving liens and trustees for Brighton in that same year.[19] Preceding the March sale, L. D. Robinson completed an updated plat and survey, recorded on March 10, 1919.[20] The very next day, on April 1, 1919, H. P. and H.W. Taylor and their wives conveyed a Deed of Trust for Brighton to E. B. Thomason and Harry Frazier, trustees, who secured a lien of $3,600 plus interest, to either Broadway National Bank or First National Bank, both in Richmond, Virginia.[21] And then, a week later, on April 7, 1919, a second Deed of Trust was arranged for the same three hundred acres of Brighton and conveyed from Hiram P. Taylor and his wife and Holcombe Taylor (wife silent) to Isaac Diggs, trustee, a well-known attorney in West Point. The deed of trust was secured at the First National Bank in Richmond, and a payment of $6,400 was evidenced by "certain interest-bearing notes." This same deed of trust stated the following: "It is understood that Roy Taylor and his wife, Annie E. Taylor, are to have a home on said farm during their natural lives or the survivor of them."[22] Such a decree would indicate that Roy and Annie were most likely the parents or grandparents of Hiram and Holcombe Taylor.

This transaction was a high price to pay for a property in King William County in 1919. At that time, the average US wage was twenty-two cents per hour, and the average US worker made between $200 and $400 per year. Two out of every ten adults could not read or write, and only 6 percent of all Americans had graduated from high school. The average life expectancy for men was forty-seven years of age. This was also during the years (1918–1920) that the Spanish Flu had infiltrated the United States, and it's possible that Roy Taylor could no longer manage the farm at Brighton without help from his extended family.

To further complicate the history of Brighton transactions that year, land records indicated that five months later, on September 4, 1919, Holcombe W. Taylor transferred his share of Brighton to Hiram P. Taylor (his brother?), and neither of the Taylor wives was mentioned in this transaction. The record noted that Holcombe conveyed his share of the bank lien and "all his rights, title, and interest" in the same three hundred acres, called Brighton.[23]

When the trustee for Brighton, attorney Isaac Diggs, died on December 3, 1922, at the age of sixty-one, the Circuit Court of King William County appointed Frank T. Sutton, Jr. of Richmond, Virginia, to take his place as trustee. Three months later, on February 1, 1923, the court convened all trustees, E. B. Thomason, Harry Frazier, Jr., and Frank T. Sutton, Jr., to discuss bankruptcy proceedings for Brighton. On April 3, 1923, the circuit court further entered a decree showing a claim from the Broadway National Bank in Richmond, Virginia, versus Hiram P. Taylor and others regarding the lien for Brighton. Records indicated that the US District Court initiated bankruptcy proceedings that same year on December 18, 1923. A few months later, in the following year, on March 30, 1924, the US District Court for the Eastern District of Virginia appointed the trustees, L. L. Sherer, Frank T. Sutton, Jr., and E. B. Thompson as special commissioners to sell Brighton, which they sold to the Broadway National Bank, due to default of liens in the amount of $3,600 and $6,400 ($10,000 total). The sale was completed on November 25, 1924 and conveyed via special warranty deed.[24]

Even though the bank in Richmond purchased Brighton as a result of foreclosure, the Taylor family was not yet done with ownership of the farm. Several months following the foreclosure sale, the wife of Holcombe W. Taylor, named Lillian Gray Taylor, purchased the "same three hundred acres" from the Broadway National Bank on April 9, 1925. For some reason, she had not been involved in Holcombe's transfer of the property to Hiram (his brother?) in 1919, and now it seemed she was able to buy Brighton back from the bank, most likely as a cash sale as there is no record of a lien or a sales price.[25] And then, four years later, on April 8, 1929, Lillian and her husband, Holcombe Taylor, sold the "same three hundred acres" known as Brighton to H. Cleveland Taylor (another relative? sibling? child?) all the while reserving the rights to *"selves, heirs, and assigns the family burying ground contained in the parcel of land hereby conveyed and an easement in the present way of approach."*[26] It's likely that the Taylor family gravesite still exists on the property at Brighton. The Kelly family discovered several gravestones near the pond spillway at the southern boundary of Brighton, and stencils (rubbings) were made by a local historian for further investigation.

Moving into the next decade, it was on September 12, 1930, that H. C. Taylor (believed to be the same as H. Cleveland Taylor) conveyed a tract of Brighton to a neighbor, A. G. Upshaw for $500 (approximately $3.50 per acre), a substantial decrease in market values in previous decades. Once again, the property at Brighton was divided into several parcels. In this transaction, Taylor sold 143 acres, three roods, and 356 sq. poles as per a survey by Francis W. Smith, a certified surveyor. The said parcel of land fronted on the old road from Aylett to Mangohick (Route 608, also known as Upshaw Road), adjoining A. G. Upshaw's property and the estate of A. C. Alexander.[27]

It was with this transaction and several others in the early 1930s that the Taylor family began to divide and sell off portions of Brighton. Since this was shortly after the stock market crash of 1929, cash was in short supply, and so, on May 4, 1931, Taylor sold another tract of land, comprising the house and outbuildings and 163.8043 acres (also surveyed by Francis W. Smith) to Mrs. Howard L. Clark (also known as Louise Jarvis Clark) of Newport, Rhode Island. It was Taylor's intention to convey all portions of Brighton farm belonging to him to Mrs. Clark. This parcel was bounded by the main road leading from Aylett to Mangohick, the lands of A. G. Upshaw,

"Cherry Hill" farm, and the property of Henry Vessels.[28] The deed noted that if the swamp bordered the southern edge of the property *"from the cedar stake, corner to A. G. Upshaw to maple at corner to Henry Vessels, the said H. Cleveland hereby grants all his rights, title and interest in the land between the straight line and the swamp to Mrs. Howard L. Clark."* It was this swampland that seeped into Aylett Creek along Brighton's southern border that was later repurposed with an earthen dam by owner Dr. Claude Kelly in 1958. With the dam, Kelly created and stocked a ten-acre bass pond, fed by dozens of fresh springs, that still exists on the property today.

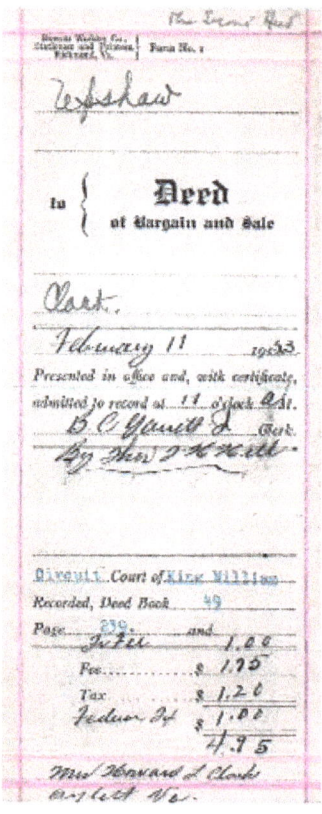

Figure 47. Deed of Trust Taylor to Upshaw. (Source: Kelly family archive)

During these recorded land transactions, the owners listed the farm at Brighton as comprising three hundred acres, more or less. It was in 1933 that the property increased in size. Another parcel of land along the farm's boundary that was "four miles above Ayletts, lying on the road running from Cattail Church to the road leading from Ayletts to Mangohick Church," which partially fronted on Route 30 (also known as the King William Highway) became part of Brighton farm during A. G. Upshaw's transactions with Mrs. Clark in 1933. This tract of 18.75 acres can be traced back to land passed from Daniel Mills to his nephew Edward (Edmund) Mills in 1866. Mills sold this small parcel for one hundred dollars ($5.33 per acre) to James T. Caldwell, a widower and a mechanic who maintained ownership for thirty years until 1896 when J. S. Moore purchased this small portion that later became part of Brighton farm.[29,30]

Moore and his wife sold these same 18.75 acres to William. D. Rouzie in 1909.[31] According to J. H. Binford, the Acting Secretary of the Virginia State Teacher's Association, Rouzie was "*a successful businessman, a man of intelligence, a staunch supporter of his school, and a man well versed in the art of fine hospitality.*" This quote was from an article titled "Snowbound in King William County," published in the *Virginia Journal of Education* in 1915. Binford had been visiting schools in King William County and became snowed in at the home of Rouzie. Instead of traveling home during a "raging blizzard," Binford wrote the following anecdote of his visit.

> Yes, things educational are prospering in King William; but the object of this article is to tell of one of the rare and happy experiences that come to us in life. On Friday, April 3 there was a teacher's meeting at Venter, and at night a big educational rally. I had counted on leaving the neighborhood early Saturday morning for Pamunkey and home. But when I awoke Saturday morning a blizzard was raging, and earth and sky filled with flurrying snow. I was in the home of Mr. W. D. Rouzie. In his sitting room was a roaring log fire; on his reading table the Literary Digest, Harper's Weekly, The North American Review, and the Times-Dispatch. On his dining table were all the good things

> to be found in our best Virginia Homes. The telephone line was down; but with our books and papers and the goodly company, including the school principal, and three teachers, one of whom was the music teacher- what difference did the isolation make? We speak of isolation in country life, but what better than the right kind of country life? We had the roaring fire, books and magazines, music and pleasant conversation. We laughed at the driving snow and counted ourselves fortunate to be snowbound. My greatest hope is that the spread of public education in Virginia may bring to pass that a home like Mr. Rouzie's will someday be the rule rather than the exception; the country home with comforts, books, music, profitable conversation, with people who have an inner mental and spiritual life, who can smile at storms in the ideal home.[32]

And so, while Mr. Rouzie and his wife Kate did not live in the house at Brighton, they owned adjacent property and typified the King William rural lifestyle. Eight years later, when Rouzie passed away at age seventy in 1917, the 18.75-acre parcel was included in Rouzie's will, with Old Dominion Trust Company named as executor.[33]

Another two years passed with Rouzie's estate in probate, and on April 19, 1919, the Trust conveyed this small parcel to Samuel Booker,[34] and two weeks later, Samuel and his wife conveyed the deed for this small parcel to J. W. Fleet, trustee. They secured a note on the property for an undisclosed amount that was to be due in twelve months, plus interest.[35] Apparently, they defaulted on the note, and a foreclosure ensued. At a public auction, the highest bid for the property was $121 (or $6.45 per acres), and thus the trustee, J. W. Fleet, conveyed the 18.75-acre tract to A. G. Upshaw on June 29, 1922.[36] And so, when Mrs. Clark began purchasing property next to Brighton farm, this tract was included with the land that A. G. Upshaw sold to her, along with the 143 acres previously noted, for a sales price of $1,000 (or about $7.00 per acre). This transaction was for the same 143 acres that Upshaw had purchased three years earlier for $3.50 per acre, or $500; and $6.21 per acre if you add in the extra tract of 18.75 acres, although it's difficult to verify the full purchase price as the receipt included acknowledgment of *"other valuable consideration paid in hand.*" By January 31, 1933, Mrs. Clark owned 321 acres, more or less, of a place called Brighton.[37] The farm boundaries remained intact until Mrs. Clark's death in 1952, except for a strip of land twenty-five feet wide, containing 50/100th of an acre, of which 30/100th was in the right of way on Route 30 and 20/100th of an acre, more or less, of additional land that Mrs. Clark transferred to the Commonwealth of Virginia for widening the roadway in May 1934.[38]

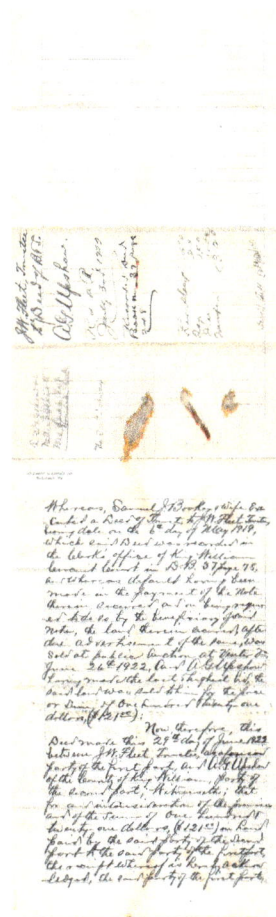

Figure 48. Deed of Trust Fleet to Upshaw. (Source: Kelly family archive]

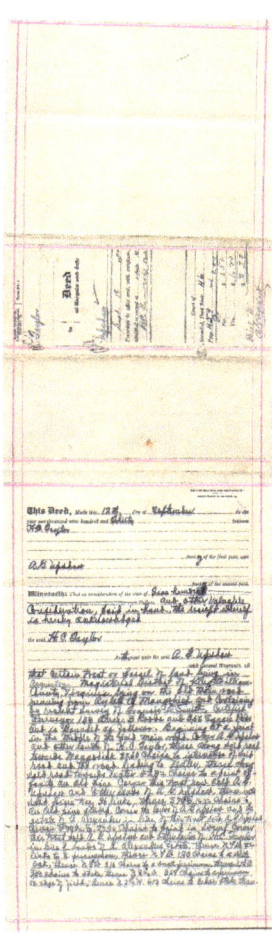

Figure 49. Deed of Trust from Upshaw to Clark. (Source: Kelly family archive)

Mrs. Howard Lee Clark (Louise Jarvis Cole), a resident of Rhode Island, purchased Brighton as a vacation property where she could raise horses and entertain her friends and relatives from New England. She owned the farm for almost two decades. During that time, she restored the house and added many modern touches, including upgrading the barn and outbuildings, to meet the needs of her horses and her frequent guests who enjoyed riding and fox hunting on the property.

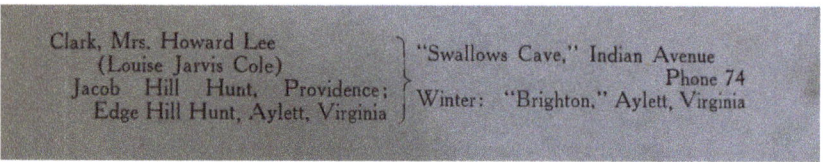

Figure 50. Mrs. Clark's Winter home Brighton. (Source: Kelly family archive)

Figure 51. Mrs. Clark's horsehead hitching posts in the front yard at Brighton. (Source: Kelly family archive)

Figure 52. The main house at Brighton with Mrs. Clark's hitching post. (Source: David Kelly)

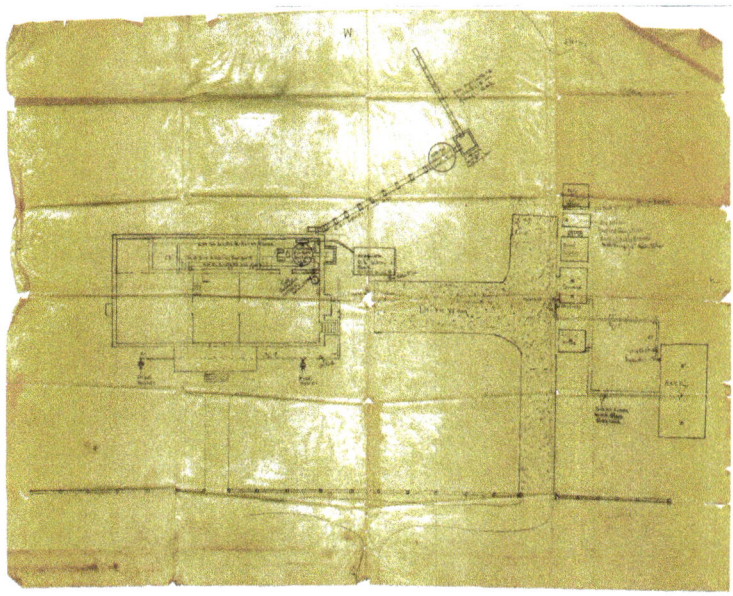

Figure 53. A sketch of Brighton Farm detailing the various utility upgrades completed by Mrs. Clark. (Source: Kelly family archive)

Some believe that Mrs. Clark was related to the family business of Coates and Clark Thread. Others have indicated that Mrs. Clark was a survivor of the *Titanic*, while her husband succumbed during the sinking in April 1912. Research evidence is lacking on both claims, even though several relics salvaged from the *Titanic* were included in Mrs. Clark's estate when Brighton was sold to Dr. Claude K. Kelly on September 29, 1952. Just one day after his thirty-second birthday, Dr. Kelly became the owner of Brighton, which comprised 330.5 acres of land, the modernized house full of furniture, dishes, and art, as well as several outbuildings and a barn that included accommodations for horses. Unlike the past decades when the property, or portions of it, were conveyed to new owners frequently, Dr. Kelly and his family would retain ownership of Brighton for the next seventy years.

Figure 54. *Dr. Kelly in the front yard at Brighton. (Photo: Kelly family archive)*

Figure 55. A view of the back of the house. (Photo: Kelly family archive)

Figure 56. A view of the front and side of the house. (Photo: Kelly family archive)

Figure 57. Brighton Aerial view. (Source: copyright Vintage Photographers, 1986 www.vintageaerial.com)

1. Atkinson, Dorothy. (1990) *King William County in the Civil War, Along Mangohick Byways.* 9. Heritage Books, Inc. MD.
2. Land Records of King William County. Deed Book 15, i281. King William County Burned Records Microfilm. Library of Virginia https://www.lva.virginia.gov/public/local/results_all.asp?CountyID=VA145
3. Atkinson, Dorothy. (1990) *King William County in the Civil War, Along Mangohick Byways.* 9, 24. Heritage Books, Inc., MD.
4. Atkinson, Dorothy. (1990) *King William County in the Civil War, Along Mangohick Byways.* 98, Heritage Books, Inc., MD.
5. Atkinson, Dorothy. (1990) *King William County in the Civil War, Along Mangohick Byways.* 24, Heritage Books, Inc., MD.
6. Atkinson, Dorothy. (1990) *King William County in the Civil War, Along Mangohick Byways.* 9, 270, Heritage Books, Inc., MD.
7. Thomas T. H. Hill, *Record of the Officers of KW County* VA, Virginia Historical Society; 1860 Census King William County.
8. Confederate States of America. Army. Dept. of Northern Virginia. Chief Engineer's Office and Blackford, B. L. (1865) *Map of King William County, Va.* [S.l.: Chief Engineer's Office, D.N.V] [Map] Retrieved from the Library of Congress, https://www.loc.gov/item/gvhs01.vhs00351/.
9. Hotchkiss, Jedediah, John Grant, A. S. Barrows, et al. *Map of King William County, Va.* 1863. Map. https://www.loc.gov/item/2002627452/.
10. King William Historical Society Newsletter October 1985. Bulletin Number 12.
11. *Richmond Times-Dispatch* Obituary Nov. 7, 1903.
12. Abstract of Title Land Deed of King William County. Deed Book 7, 204.
13. Chataigne's *Virginia Gazetteer and Classified Business Directory* 1888–1889. King William County https://www.newrivernotes.com/topical_business_1888_chataigne_gazetteer.htm#KingWilliam

14. Abstract of Title Land Deeds of King William County. Deed Book 7, 204.
15. Zontine, Patricia. (April 2009) Dr. Thomas Walker (1714–1794). Jefferson Library. Monticello. https://www.monticello.org/sites/library/exhibits/lucymarks/lucymarks/bios/drthomaswalker.html
16. Ball, Bonnie. (1978) *Dr. Thomas Walker. Historical Sketches of Southwest Virginia.* The Historical Society of Southwest Virginia, publication 12, 5–9. http://sites.rootsweb.com/~vahsswv/historicalsketches/walker%20drthomas.html
17. *Abstract of Title Land Deeds of King William County* Deed Book 9, 282.
18. *Abstract of Title Land Deeds of King William County* Deed Book 15, 220.
19. *Abstract of Title Land Deeds of King William County* Deed Book 34, 165.
20. *Abstract of Title Land Deeds of King William County* Deed Book 34, 166.
21. *Abstract of Title Land Deeds of King William County* Deed Book 34, 167.
22. *Abstract of Title Land Deeds of King William County* Deed Book 35, 14.
23. *Abstract of Title Land Deeds of King William County* Deed Book 34, 497.
24. *Abstract of Title Land Deeds of King William County* Deed Book 40, 186.
25. *Abstract of Title Land Deeds of King William County* Deed Book 40, 374.
26. *Abstract of Title Land Deeds of King William County* Deed Book 45, 118.
27. *Abstract of Title Land Deeds of King William County* Deed Book 46, 459.
28. *Abstract of Title Land Deeds of King William County* Deed Book 47, 429.

29. Land Records of King William County. Deed Book 16, i421. King William County Burned Records Microfilm. Library of Virginia.
30. *Abstract of Title Land Deeds of King William County* Deed Book 14, 310.
31. *Abstract of Title Land Deeds of King William County* Deed Book 23, 529.
32. Binford, J.H. (1915) "Snowbound in King William." The Virginia Journal of Education. Vol. 8. 495.
33. *Abstract of Title Land Deeds of King William County* Will Book 2, 119.
34. *Abstract of Title Land Deeds of King William County* Deed Book 34, 252.
35. *Abstract of Title Land Deeds of King William County* Deed Book 37, 78.
36. *Abstract of Title Land Deeds of King William County* Deed Book 37, 248.
37. *Abstract of Title Land Deeds of King William County* Deed Book 49, 429.
38. *Abstract of Title Land Deeds of King William County* Deed Book 50, 479.

CHAPTER V
Brighton, the Most Recent Years 1952 to 2021

"The loss of my mother when I was not yet two years old and my father when I was ten resulted in childhood memories gleaned from stories of their lives, as recalled by relatives and family friends. It's clear from their photos that they shared a deep love for each other, for their family and for their farm at Brighton. It's always comforting when I see glimpses of their smiles in the faces of my siblings, my children and my grandchildren."

Figure 58. Brighton overhead view of the house, pond and red barn. (Source: Kelly family archive)

Figure 59. Brighton Sky view. View of Brighton Farm from the west. (Source: Kelly family archive)

Figure 60. View of the house from the lane. (Source: Kelly family archive)

Figure 61. House with white fence. (Source: Kelly family archive]

Mrs. Howard L. Clark, also known as Louise Jarvis Clark, was a widow who traveled from her home in Middletown, Rhode Island, to Aylett, Virginia, to visit her farm at Brighton. During the twenty years after purchasing the property in 1931, she made improvements to the house, filling it with paintings and furniture befitting a fine, restored Virginia home. Here she enjoyed hosting her family and friends from New England, who ventured south for horseback riding and to escape the cold northern winters. When she died in late 1951, the named executors of her estate were her sister, Alice, and the Rhode Island Hospital Trust Company. Her will, probated on January 23, 1952, specified, "*I give and devise to my sister, Alice Bradford Ransom, all of my real estate and personal property located in Aylett, in the state of Virginia.*"[1] Her sister, Alice, also a widow, listed the farm for sale, and, on September 29, 1952, Dr. Claude Kelso Kelly, a young physician with a practice in nearby Hanover County, purchased Brighton. It was an estate sale, which included much of the household furnishings, antiques, paintings, etc., along with the house, outbuildings, and 321 acres, more or less. Dr. Kelly had recently assumed responsibility for the medical practice of his mentor, Dr. Israel Kay Redd I, near Mechanicsville, Virginia, about thirty miles away from Brighton. On learning of his new purchase, he contacted his friend, Chaney Carlton, an insurance and car salesman, and said, "*Hey, let's go see what I've just bought!*" And at that point, he became a gentleman farmer, as well as a country doctor.

The land deed described the property as several adjoining tracts of land in Acquinton Magisterial District, King William County, Virginia, known as Brighton, containing 321 acres. In 1952, the assessed value of the buildings was $2,660, and the value of the two tracts of 162 and 168.5 acres (which actually equaled 330.5 acres) was $4,930 plus $125.24 in taxes, for a total assessed property value of $7,715, or $24.00 per acre.[2] Dr. Kelly obtained a note on the property from Southside Bank in Aylett for $22,000 and conveyed the deed of trust to attorney Douglas S. Mitchell, trustee. The first lien of a deed of trust of $2,200 was also recorded on October 17, 1952; however, the actual sales price was not listed on the deed of trust.[3]

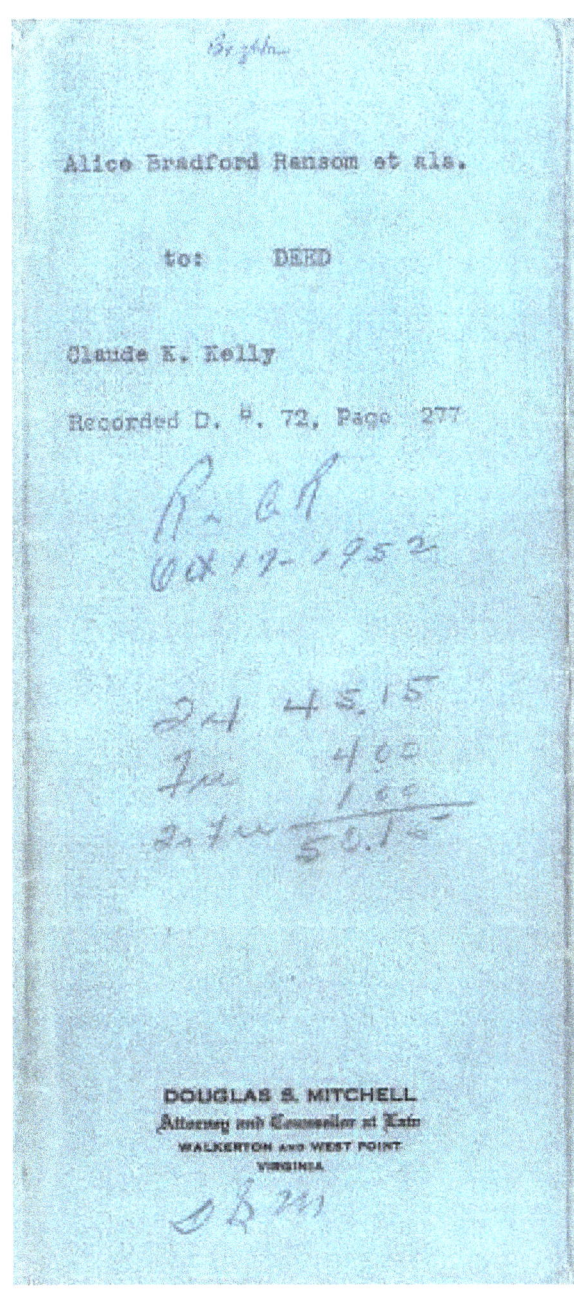

Figure 62. Deed for Brighton recorded in Deed Book 72, page 277. Seller: Alice Bradford Ransom, Buyer: Dr. Claude Kelso Kelly. (Source: Kelly family archive)

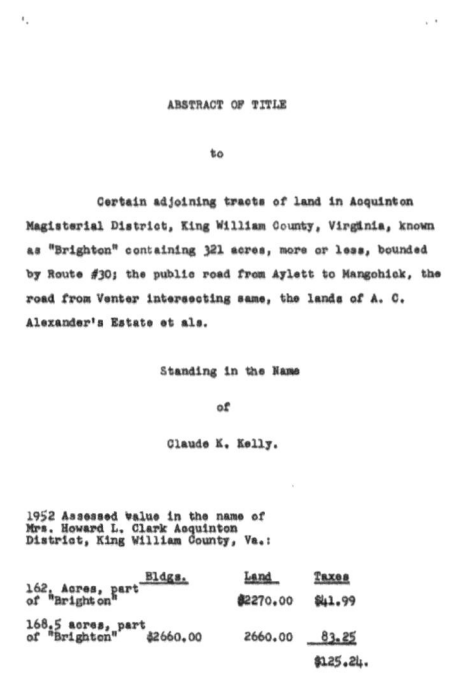

Figure 63. Abstract of Title for Brighton from May 9, 1888 to October 3, 1952. (Source: Kelly family archive)

Today, by comparison, some seventy years later, the King William County 2021 reassessment of the property, now comprising 305.69 acres, noted an assessed land value of $830,500 and the value of the buildings as $367,900 for a total assessed value of $1,198,400, or $3,920 per acre. The reduction in total acreage was because of the sale of fifteen acres along Brighton's western boundary by Kelly's second wife, Eva Jo Kelly. She developed "Brighton Forest" by selling a dozen one-acre lots to home builders in 1990. One of the lots is still available for sale in 2021, with a county assessed value of $25,000. This remaining one-acre lot on Beadles Lane borders Brighton at the southwestern boundary of the property. It's clear that property values in King William County have increased significantly over the years.[4]

The description of the property in 1952 noted that the property comprised:

> All that tract of land with buildings and improvements thereon called Brighton containing 321 acres, more or less, but sold and conveyed in gross and not by the acre, and consists of three adjoining tracts or parcels of three adjoining tracts or parcels, as follows:
>
> FIRST: A tract of land being a part of Brighton containing 159.79 acres, more or less, bounded by the main road leading from Aylett to Mangohick, "Cherry Hill" Farm, other lands which Louise Jarvis Clark died seized, the lands of Junius Diggs and Mary Diggs et als; It being all of that tract of land conveyed to Louise Jarvis Clark in the name of Mrs. Howard L. Clark by deed dated May 4, 1931 from H. Cleveland Taylor... EXCEPT 4.01 acres thereof conveyed Junius Diggs and Mary Diggs by deed dated June 23, 1952 from Alice Bradford Ransom.
>
> SECOND: (a) A tract of land being a part of Brighton containing 143 acres, 3 roods and 356 sq. rods bounded by the main road leading from Upshaw to Mangohick and by road leading from Venter which intersects same...being all of the same property conveyed A.G. Upshaw by deed dated December 12, 1930 from H.C. Taylor;
>
> (b) A tract supposed to contain 18.25 acres, more or less, bounded by Route #30 leading from Venter towards Mangohick, the lands of A.C. Alexander's estate and other lands which Louise Jarvis Clark, died seized, et als; it being the same land conveyed A.G. Upshaw by deed from J.W. Fleet, Trustee, dated June 29, 1922.[5]

The four acres conveyed to the Diggs family was a parcel to the east of the property. For many years, Junius and Mary Diggs provided maintenance support and other services to Mrs. Clark, and as her closest neighbors, they may have looked after the property in her absence. At any rate, in 1952, Dr. Kelly received clear title to the farm, and the Kelly family continued to own Brighton for the next seventy years.

Claude Kelso Kelly was born September 28, 1920, to Herbert Willis Kelly (1900–1957) and Cecelia Bee Hefler (born July 26, 1902, in Bruington, King and Queen County). His parents married on June 13, 1917, just a month before Cecelia celebrated her fifteenth birthday. They had five children, three of whom died in 1924. One child died at one year of age, another was a month old, and the third, a newborn, was only one day old. And so only Claude and his older sister, Katrina Rosalind "Kitty (born August 3, 1919), survived. For a time, Herbert Kelly worked as a streetcar conductor in Niagara Falls, New York. It was here that Herbert changed his last name from "Kelley" to "Kelly" because of "heated disagreements" and altercations with other Kelley relatives that he did not want to associate with.

Figure 64. Claude as a young boy with his mother Cecelia and older sister Kitty. (Source: Kelly family archive)

Herbert and Cecelia's marriage lasted eleven years, and they divorced on March 4, 1928, when Claude was seven years old. Claude and Kitty attended elementary school in Baltimore. After the divorce,

Herbert married Dorothy Roane (1910–2000), and Claude and his sister, "Kitty," a year older, would spend time traveling between their divorced parents' homes in Baltimore and New York. Cecelia would go on to marry twice more. First to Frank Ferrara, an Italian Catholic (her words) and widower with five young children. During this marriage, Claude and Kitty lived with their father and attended school in Niagara Falls. Cecelia and Frank divorced after six or seven years, and Cecelia then married Harry Cartwright, who had been a cook in the navy and was from Des Moines, Iowa. He worked in Baltimore as a dry cleaner and died in 1948. Prior to that marriage, Claude and Kitty had returned to Virginia to attend Central High School in King William County. Claude graduated in 1938. He and Kitty spent most of their growing-up years on a farm not far from Brighton with their grandmother, Martha "Mattie" Claiborne Wilson Kelley (1878–1944), and their grandfather, Edward "Eddie" Burton Kelley (1871–1940). Their gravesites, along with many other Kelly and Kelley relatives, are in the cemetery at Sharon Baptist Church in King William County.

Figure 65. *Claude and his sister Katrina (Kitty)*. (Source: Kelly family archive)

Figure 66. Cecelia Bee Cartwright, Claude's mother. (Source: Kelly family archive)

Figure 67. Cecilia Cartwright, grandmother to the Kelly children, who helped care for them after their mother's death in 1957. (Source: Kelly family archive)

Figure 68. Gravestones of Claude's grandparents, Eddie Burton and Martha Wilson Kelley at Sharon Baptist Church cemetery near Central Garage in King William Virginia. (Source: Kelly family archive)

The elder Herbert Kelly, Sr. and his second wife Dorothy later settled on a farm known as Presque Isle in King William County, about eight miles from Brighton. Herbert and Dorothy had two more children, Herbert Kelly, Jr. (1931–2000), who graduated from Virginia Tech University and became a prominent veterinarian in Newport News, Virginia, and Dolores Mae Montalban of Columbia Heights, Virginia, who maintained the farm at Presque Isle after Dorothy's death.

Claude and his siblings enjoyed spending time on Presque Isle, which occupied a bend on the Mattaponi River, where Claude taught swimming lessons to local children. Excelling at all sports in high school, Claude attended the College of William and Mary in Williamsburg, Virginia, where he ran track, having spent many years chasing rabbits across the fields on the farm in King William. At least, that's the story he later told the Kelly children. Following graduation from college, Kelly attended the Medical College of

Virginia in Richmond and received his MD in June 1945. He received a commission as lieutenant in the United States Medical Corps, and he accepted an appointment at the United States Naval Hospital in Bainbridge, Maryland, where he completed his residency.

Figure 69. Claude Kelso Kelly in Navy Uniform (Source: Kelly family archive)

Figure 70. Claude Kelly, pictured on the far left, and fellow medical students at the Medical College of Virginia in Richmond, Virginia. (Source: Kelly family archive)

Figure 71. Dr. Claude Kelso Kelly during his commission as lieutenant in the United States Medical Corp at the US Navy Hospital in Bainbridge, Maryland. (Source: Kelly family archive)

Following his residency, Dr. Kelly and another young physician, Dr. Edwin "Ned" Wysor, joined the medical practice of Dr. Israel Kay Redd I in Hanover County, Virginia. Kelly, fresh out of medical school and the navy, and Wysor, or "Doc," a graduate of the University of Virginia Medical School and the Army Medical Corps during World War II, lived at the home of their mentor, Dr. Redd, where he also had his medical office, a common practice for doctors at the time.

When Dr. Redd died in August 1948, at the age of fifty-five, Wysor and Kelly continued serving his patients in their rural homes. Dr. Redd's medical practice had peaked at the transition of "horse and buggy" doctors. In the mid-twentieth century, the increase in automobiles, the spread of electricity to rural areas, and the increase in pharmacists had led to the establishment of doctor's offices and medical clinics in the region. Dr. Redd's daughter, Jane Carroll Redd Dunford, recalled: *"her father's thirty-three years of practice... of calls by horse and buggy and by car, of one-dollar office visits, of delivering more than two thousand babies (mostly at home) and of the wonder at the 'miracle drugs' available by the 1940s."*[6] There are stories of Wysor and Kelly, both bachelors, taking turns leaping out of bed in the middle of the night to attend to medical emergencies in patients' homes. One story that was often repeated was the night that "Doc" Wysor, who was well over six feet tall, rushed out to deliver a baby and realized too late that he had worn Claude's pants, which were significantly shorter due to Kelly's much smaller five-feet, six-inch frame. A short time later, the two young doctors, with the help of the local community, established the Mechanicsville Medical Center Family Practice, which is still in operation today, over seventy years later.[7] The medical center would soon expand to include four physicians and a dentist, Dr. Theodore Crowe. Kelly continued to see patients there for seventeen years until his death in September 1965. Dr. Kelly's granddaughter, Madison, interned briefly at the medical center as part of her nurse training in 2020.

Figure 72. December 1960 Staff Christmas Card from the Mechanicsville Medical Center. Pictured from lower left: Dr. Ned "Doc" Wysor, Dr. Kelly, Dr. Theodore Crowe; from upper left: Louise Kinker, Clara Basker, Nancy Lynch, Hazel Mann, Patsy Setzer and Georgie Granger. (Source: Kelly family archive)

Figure 73. Mechanicsville Medical Center Physicians. Pictured from lower left: Dr. Ned "Doc" Wysor, Dr. Bowers, Dr. Kelly; Upper Left: Dr. Crowe, Dr. Evans, Dr. Harlow. (Source: Kelly family archive)

Figure 74. Claude's sister Kitty Smallwood and his mother Cecelia Cartwright at Brighton. (Photo: Kelly family archive)

Figure 75. Dr. Kelly and his mother, Cecelia Cartwright in the front yard at Brighton. (Source: Kelly family archive)

Figure 76. Claude and his mother, Cecelia Cartwright sitting under the grape arbor in the backyard at Brighton. (Source: Kelly family archive)

Figure 77. Dr. Kelly and his new car in the front yard at Brighton. (Source: Kelly family archive)

Figure 78. Dr. Kelly and his two hunting dogs in the side yard at Brighton. (Source: Kelly family archive)

Figure 79. Black Angus in the field at Brighton, October 1954. (Source: Kelly family archive)

Not long after the establishment of the medical center, Kelly met a nursing student, Nettie Virginia Joyner, of Ivor, Virginia. Nettie graduated from St. Luke's Hospital School of Nursing in Richmond, Virginia, in June 1953. On October 9, 1953, she married Dr. Kelly, thirteen years her senior, at the First Baptist Church in Richmond. They settled on the farm at Brighton, which was isolated, compared to the small town of Ivor where Nettie grew up. She was born during the Great Depression in 1933 on a farm where her father, Crawford, worked in the Isle of Wight County in Virginia. When she was six years old, her father stopped farming and worked as a carpenter when work was available. When she was ten, the family moved to Ivor, in Southampton County, and her father found carpentry work at the shipyards and later died in 1958 from injuries suffered in an accident on the job years earlier. After his shipyard accident, Nettie's mother, Elizabeth, known as "Miss Lizzie," cared for Crawford while raising their seven children: Merle, Nettie, Massey, Josie, Gloria, C.B., and Linda. Except for Gloria—a retired teacher who now lives on a cattle ranch in Geronimo, Oklahoma, with her retired military husband, Dan—all the Joyner siblings still reside in the Ivor area. Mrs. "Lizzie" Joyner suffered from heart disease most of her life and died in 2001 from congestive heart failure.

Figure 80. Nettie Virginia Joyner. (Source: Kelly family archive)

Figure 81. Nettie Virginia Joyner at Brighton. (Source: Kelly family archive)

Figure 82. Nettie Joyner, aged 16, in Ivor, Virginia 1949. (Source: Kelly family archive)

Figure 83. Nettie Joyner in her middle school band uniform. (Source: Kelly family archive)

Figure 84. Nettie Joyner's nursing school graduation class, St. Luke's Hospital, June 1953. (Source: Kelly family archive)

Figure 85. Nettie and Claude at her graduation from St. Luke's Hospital School of Nursing in Richmond, Virginia, June 1953. (Source: Kelly family archive)

Figure 86. Nettie and Claude's Wedding Day 1953. (Source: Kelly family archive)

Figure 87. Claude, Nettie and best man, Chainey Carlton at their wedding in 1953. (Source: Kelly family archive)

Figure 88. Claude, Nettie, best man, Chainey Carlton and maid of honor, Merle Joyner, at Claude and Nettie's wedding in October 1953. (Source: Kelly family archive)

Figure 89. Claude and Nettie's wedding. Pictured from left: Vernon Smallwood, Kitty Smallwood, Phyllis Smallwood, Cecelia Cartwright, Nettie, Claude, Dolores Kelly, Dorothy Kelly, Herbert Kelly. (Source: Kelly family archive)

Figure 90. Claude and Nettie's wedding. Pictured from left: Crawford Joyner, Merle Joyner, Elizabeth "Lizzie" Joyner, Nettie, Claude, Josie Joyner, Virginia Joyner West, Margaret Joyner. (Source: Kelly family archive)

Figure 91. Claude and Nettie in the car on their wedding day. (Kelly family archive)

Figure 92. Claude and Nettie. Just Married 1953. (Source: Kelly family archive)

Figure 93. Dr. Kelly, Uncle Vernon Smallwood and Chainey Carlton playing horseshoes in the backyard at Brighton. (Source: Kelly family archive)

With Claude away most days working at the medical center, Nettie decided she needed to learn to drive, and she used Brighton's long, sandy lane leading to the property for practice. According to the Joyner siblings, there used to be several large trees at the entrance to the farm, which was soon removed to improve visibility and to reduce damages to the car by the novice driver.

In addition to his medical practice and raising Black Angus cattle at Brighton, Nettie and Claude wanted a family, and they had three children in the next three years. Claude Kelso Kelly, Jr. was born in September 1954, Karen Leigh Kelly in July 1955, and Paula Kay Kelly in October 1956. Several times a month, Nettie would drive, with the three young Kelly children, to visit her parents and six siblings in Ivor, about three hours away. Sadly, her years at the farm were short-lived, and at the age of twenty-four, she suffered a cerebral hemorrhage on March 11, 1957. She collapsed and died minutes after a phone call from Claude, who had called her at Brighton to let her know about her father-in-law, Herbert Kelly's heart attack and death at nearby Presque Isle earlier that day. Elizabeth, who was working at the house that day, collected the three young children and raced across the fields to the nearby Diggs home to seek help.

Figure 94. Dr. Kelly and his son, Claude, Jr. 1954. (Source: Kelly family archive)

Figure 95. Karen (the author of A Place Called Brighton) and her brother, Claude, Jr. in the front yard at Brighton. (Source: Kelly family archive)

Figure 96. Claude, Jr., Karen and Paula in the living room at Brighton XMAS 1956. (Source: Kelly family archive)

Joint Services For Heart Victims Set

AYLETT, March 12.—Joint funeral services will be held tomorrow for a King William county man and his daughter-in-law, both of whom died yesterday of heart attacks within a few minutes of each other.

Herbert W. Kelly, 51, a farmer, died at his home, about eight miles from the home of his son, Dr. Claude K. Kelly. Dr. Kelly's wife, upon learning of Mr. Kelly's death, suffered a heart attack and died shortly after.

The services will be held at 3 p.m. at the West Funeral Home, Mechanicsville, with burial in Sharon Baptist Church Cemetery, King William county.

Besides her husband, Mrs. Kelly is survived by two daughters, Misses Karen Lee and Paula Kay Kelly; a son, Claude K. Kelly Jr.; her parents, Mr. and Mrs. Crawford Joyner; four sisters, Misses Merle, Josie, Gloria and Linda Sue Joyner, and two brothers, Massie and C. B. Joyner, all of Ivor, Southampton county.

Besides Dr. Kelly, Mr. Kelly is survived by his wife, Mrs. Dorothy Roane Kelly; another son, Dr. Herbert Kelly Jr. of Arlington; two daughters, Mrs. Katrina Smallwood of Baltimore, Md. and Mrs. Delores Mae Montalbano of Colonial Heights; a sister, Mrs. Hattie Gallagher of Portsmouth, Va., and a brother, John B. Kelly, West Point and six gradnchildren.

Figure 97. Herbert Kelly and Nettie Kelly obituary March 12, 1957. Even though the headline reads that both suffered heart attacks, Nettie actually died of a cerebral aneurysm at the age of 24. (Source: Kelly family archive)

Figure 98. Claude, Jr. (Kelso) on his new tractor in the front yard at Brighton. (Source: Kelly family archive)

Figure 99. Claude, Jr. and Karen in April after their mother, Nettie's, death in March 1957. (Source: Kelly family archive)

Heartbroken, with three young children ages five months (Kay), twenty months (Karen), and two-and-a-half years (Claude, Jr.), Dr. Kelly resisted offers from his siblings, Kitty, Herbert, and Dolores, that they each adopt one of the children. In need of support for his children and determined that they be raised together, he convinced his mother, Cecelia, to move from her home in Baltimore, Maryland, to come and live with his young family at Brighton. He believed this was the best choice for everyone, as he continued to develop the farm and manage his medical practice in Mechanicsville. Cecelia was not happy about living in the same county as Herbert's second wife, Dorothy, whom she blamed for her divorce from Herbert years before. She claimed that even though Herbert *"was a mean drunk, he was also the love of [her] life."* And yet, for the next few years, she lived at Brighton and did her best to care for the three young Kelly children with the daily help of housekeepers Elizabeth Garlick and Rosa Vessels, who lived nearby.

Still grieving the loss of Nettie and his father, who had died tragically on the same day, Claude continued to maintain his medical practice, working long hours on call and often having a meal or resting at the home of friends in Mechanicsville, who lived near the medical center. One such couple who enjoyed looking after Claude was Earle and Marjorie Eubank and their young daughter, Sallie Mann. It was at their home for dinner one evening that they introduced Claude to Eva Jo Liskey Dobbins, a young widow whose husband Reid had recently drowned while on a boating outing in the Rappahannock River. Eva Jo, a graduate of James Madison University in Harrisonburg, Virginia, was eleven years younger than Claude and worked as a home economist at the Virginia Electric and Power Company in Richmond. Eva Jo was one of seven children and the oldest daughter of David and Evangeline Liskey, who lived on a farm in Harrisonburg, Virginia, in the Shenandoah Valley. Not long after they met, Eva Jo began to accompany Claude on house calls when he was working in the evenings in Hanover County. Having no children from her first marriage, Jo soon became a familiar guest at Brighton, often to the dismay of Grandmother Cartwright.

Figure 100. Dr. Kelly and Eva Jo Liskey, 1961. (Source: Kelly family archive)

Figure 101. Eva Jo Liskey. (Source: Kelly family archive)

Figure 102. Eva Jo Liskey Kelly. (Source: Kelly family archive)

Figure 103. Dr. Kelly and Eva Jo eating crabs at a local restaurant. (Source: Kelly family archive)

Claude and Eva Jo married in November 1960, honeymooned at Niagara Falls, and in September 1961, they welcomed two more children, twins David Keith and Earl Kevin, to the Kelly family. Brighton became a very busy household. Prior to the birth of the twins, Cecelia had returned to Baltimore, as she and Eva Jo did not always agree on the care of the children, and Claude was concerned that the constant tension was not good for the pregnancy. The day he drove her to the bus station with her suitcases in what might have been a somber goodbye for the Kelly children turned into a celebration as Eva Jo exclaimed, "Who wants ice cream?"

Figure 104. Dr. Kelly and Eva Jo in the living room at Brighton. (Source: Kelly family archive)

Figure 105. Dr. Kelly, Eva Jo and family in the living room at Brighton, 1961. (Source: Kelly family archive)

Figure 106. Kelly family 1964. (Source: Kelly family archive)

Eva Jo and Claude were fortunate to have daily housekeepers and hired farmhands to help support their young family and the cattle farm. Dr. Kelly took a day off in the middle of each week to tend to his expanding Black Angus herd. He also needed more time to manage his farms at Edgehill and Octagon and the rental houses and log cabin at the Aylett Millpond, near Presque Isle, which catered to various fishing clubs over the years. Kelly, an avid fisherman, also developed a ten-acre bass pond in the swampy, spring fed-portion of the farm at Brighton. Friends and relatives often visited to enjoy fresh-caught fish and Eva Jo's southern cooking. It was a common occurrence for Dr. Kelly to load up the children in the station wagon and go for a drive to collect rent at the farms, view the herds of cattle (challenging Claude, Jr., Karen, and Kay to see how many they could count), stopping to chat with neighbors, or pick up a few items at Chenault's General Store in Aylett.

Figure 107. Dr. Kelly, Eva Jo, David Kelly and David Liskey, Eva Jo's father, after a visit with her parents at Brighton. (Source: Kelly family archive)

Figure 108. David and Earl playing in the fenced in front yard at Brighton. (Source: Kelly family archive)

Figure 109. David and Earl with Dr. Kelly in the basement at Brighton. (Source: Kelly family archive)

Besides his medical practice and farming, Kelly continued to invest in real estate, and one investment that paid off was the sale of the property he owned at Doswell, Virginia, just off the exit from I-95. This area soon developed into a thriving truck stop and an amusement park, known as "Kings Dominion," which still caters to crowds today. As teenagers, all five Kelly children had summer jobs at the park, which was about twenty miles west of Brighton.

Despite a full schedule with work and family, Dr. Kelly was active in the community, serving as a deacon at Sharon Baptist Church. As an enthusiastic baseball fan (and especially the New York Yankees), he was instrumental in the planning and construction of the King William County Recreation Park for families in the community. Here the Kelly children participated in softball and baseball, often with their father as a coach or cheering from the bleachers. His appreciation of water sports led him to help design, develop, and serve on the board of the Mechanicsville Recreation Association, Inc., where the Kelly children enjoyed swimming every summer, down the road from their father's medical practice.[8] Throughout his life, Dr. Kelly was a member of the American Medical Association, the Virginia Medical Society, and Omicron Delta Kappa, a national leadership honor society, "recognizing superior leadership and exemplary character," which he was accepted into during his college days at William and Mary. At one point, he served as president of the local Parent-Teacher Association (PTA) for King William County public schools, where all five Kelly children attended elementary school. In 1962, he and his medical team administered the Sabin polio vaccine to all the elementary children (including his own) in the cafeteria of the local school. As one of the few doctors in the county, he often saw patients in the back hallway of the house at Brighton. He treated childhood illnesses, earaches, colds, and farm accidents from the enclosed back porch. On one occasion, the removal of a piece of corn that had sprouted in a youngster's nose was followed with a stern reminder to all the Kelly children to never attempt such a thing.

Life at Brighton for the Kelly children was a whirlwind of activity and outdoor experiences. Horseshoes, touch football, kick-the-can games in the twilight, fishing (always wearing life jackets!), swimming, canoeing around the lily pads, jumping into piles of hay from the barn loft, bicycling out the lane to the school bus, collecting bugs, cracking English walnuts, pony rides, adventures in the woods, turning huge fallen tree trunks into spaceships and sailing vessels, orange Hi-C and peanut butter and jelly sandwiches under the shade of trees in the yard, catching lightning bugs in jars, falling asleep to the sound of crickets chirping (before air conditioning), swatting mosquitos, mowing the grass, smelling the daffodils and magnolias, ice skating (on the small ice pond used to collect ice in colonial days), piano lessons, library books, 4-H, scouts, hunting, Saturday chores and Sunday school, Vacation Bible School, and countless visits from friends and relatives who enjoyed spending time at Brighton. Frequent guests were Claude's sister, Kitty, and her husband, Vernon Smallwood, and their two children, Phyllis (Gibson) and Lee. The Smallwood family never failed to delight the Kelly kids with boxes of doughnuts from Baltimore, and they had hardly unpacked before they headed to the pond to fish for hours and hours.

Other guests included the extended family members of the Liskeys, as Eva Jo was one of seven siblings. The Liskey brothers—David, Jimmy, Richard, Al, and John Stephen—all traveled with their wives and children from Harrisonburg, Virginia, to spend time at Brighton. Eva Jo's only sister, Laura Lynne, became a favorite overnight guest and babysitter for the Kelly children while she attended college nearby in Richmond.

It was during the first few months of 1965 that Dr. Kelly learned he was suffering from an advanced stage of liver cancer. Being fully aware of the unlikely success of any treatment, he opted to spend his last days at Brighton, managing his farm and spending time with his family. He organized his affairs, which by now included many properties and assets. He named Eva Jo, his wife of fewer than five years, the executor of his estate. Following his death at Brighton in

September 1965, which, at his request, was medically assisted by his friend, "Doc" Wysor, there were several planned sales and auctions of real estate, cattle, and farm equipment that helped to ensure the financial security of the Kelly family.

Figure 110. Dr. Kelly with Paula, Karen and the twins in the front yard at Brighton. (Source: Kelly family archive)

Figure 111. Kelly kids on the monkey bars in the front yard at Brighton, September 1965. (Source: Kelly family archive)

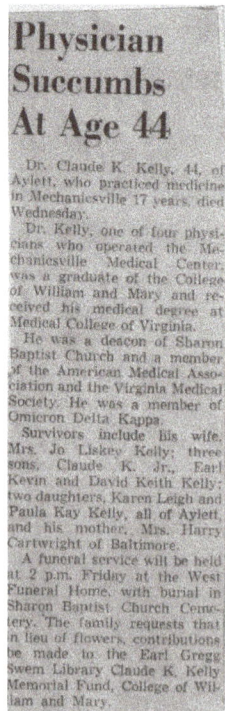

Figure 112. Dr. Claude Kelso Kelly's obituary September 1965. (Source: Kelly family archive)

Figure 113. Claude, Jr., Paula and Karen celebrating Claude Jr.'s birthday in the basement at Brighton. (Source: Kelly family archive)

Figure 114. Claude and Nettie's gravestones at Sharon Baptist Church in King William County. (Source: Kelly family archive)

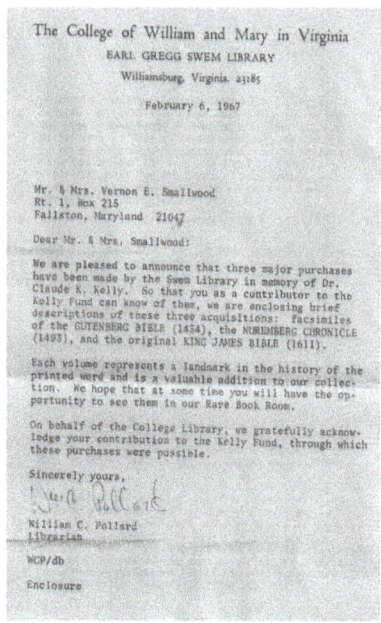

Figure 115. In memory of Dr. Kelly. This letter from Dr. Kelly's alma mater, the College of William and Mary, describes the three rare books purchased with memorial funds and added to the collection at the Earl Gregg Swem Library. These books can be viewed by appointment at the College Library. (Source: Kelly family archive)

Figure 116. Dinner in the basement at Brighton with family and friends. Pictured back row left: Aunt Kitty Smallwood, David, Eva Jo, Earl Eubank, Cecelia Cartwright; front: Earl and Marjorie Eubank. (Source: Kelly family archive)

Figure 117. Kelso, Karen, Earl and David at the Mechanicsville pool. (Source: Kelly family archive)

Figure 118. Miss Lizzie (Grandmother Joyner) and grandchildren on her front porch in Ivor, Virginia. Top row from the left: Keith Joyner, David Kelly, "Miss Lizzie" Joyner with Jeffrey Parker on her lap, Kelso (Claude, Jr.) Second row from the left: Earl Kelly, Karen Kelly with Jeannette Parker on her lap, Paula Kelly with Karen Joyner on her lap. (Source: Kelly family archive)

Figure 119. Eva Jo and the Kelly kids in the pony cart at the end of the lane at Brighton. (Source: Kelly family archive)

Figure 120. The Kelly kids enjoying a ride in the pony cart with Eva Jo. Grandfather David Liskey provided the pony and the cart in the fall of 1965. (Source: Kelly family archive)

Figure 121. Kelly kids with Elizabeth's family who were visiting to ride the pony. (Source: Kelly family archive)

Figure 122. Darren Gibson, Uncle Vernon Smallwood, Kevin Gibson and Dennis Gibson always enjoyed fishing at Brighton. (Source: Kelly family archive)

A PLACE CALLED BRIGHTON

Figure 123. Kelso, Vernon and Lee Smallwood and Steve Liskey spent many early mornings fishing at Brighton. (Source: Kelly family archive)

Figure 124. Kelly kids with the Smallwood and Gibson families in the front yard at Brighton. (Source: Kelly family archive)

Figure 125. Karen, Lee Smallwood, Kelso, David, Earl and Paula playing touch football in the back yard at Brighton. (Source: Kelly family archive)

Figure 126. A human pyramid in the front yard at Brighton. Pictured from top to bottom, left to right: David, Karen, Paula, Kelso, Lee Smallwood, Steve Liskey and Earl. (Source: Kelly family archive)

Figure 127. The Smallwood family pictured with the Kelly kids after attending church one spring Sunday. Back row, left to right: Cecelia Cartwright, Karen, Dennis Gibson, Kelso, Vernon Smallwood; Front row, left to right: Paula, Kitty Smallwood, Phyllis (Smallwood) Gibson holding on to Earl and David and little Darren Gibson in the front. (Source: Kelly family archive)

Figure 128. Kelso about to go squirrel hunting at Brighton. (Source: Kelly family archive)

Eva Jo's promise to Claude was to focus on the children's education and to manage his estate so that they could all grow up at Brighton. And for the most part, they did. However, several years after Claude's death, Eva Jo moved the family to Henrico County so that the children could attend schools that were still segregated. Even though it was more than a decade after the US Supreme Court ruled on school equality in Brown v. the Board of Education (1954), the tensions in the King William County public schools were her primary concern. Throughout Virginia, busing was being instituted to help equalize the racial makeup of schools and to provide improved academic opportunities for all children. The resistance to integration in Virginia was intense for both the black and white communities.[9] Desegregation was often debated in the Virginia legislature as in the statement from then Virginia Senator Mills E. Goodwin, Jr., who said in 1956, *"Integration, however slight, anywhere in Virginia would be a cancer eating at the very life blood of our public school system."*[10] A staunch opponent of desegregation, Goodwin would serve as Virginia's governor from 1966 to 1970 and from 1974 to 1978 and was often referred to as "the education governor." During Goodwin's first term in office, another senator nominated Claude, Jr. (Kelso), then a young teen, to serve as a Senate page for the Virginia legislative sessions.

It was not long before tensions over integration caused significant disruptions in Henrico and Richmond Public Schools, and so Eva Jo decided to move the family back to Brighton in the summer of 1971. She remodeled and updated the kitchen with yellow floors, orange countertops, and blue cabinets, moving it from the basement to a compact addition on the back of the house and added another bathroom and laundry/sewing room. Since the schools were still struggling with integration in King William County, she opted to enroll all the children in private schools. Actually, they enrolled in four different private schools.

Kelso (his middle and preferred name, rather than Claude, Jr.) attended Hargrave Military Academy in Chatam, Virginia, and graduated in 1972. He was admitted to the College of William and Mary and attended for two years as a pre-med student, following in his father's footsteps. After a spring skiing visit to see Karen, who was attending the University of Colorado in Boulder (CU-B), he decided to transfer there and graduated two years later with a degree in business. After graduation, Kelso, a talented musician, put his business degree to good use by joining and managing a rock band and spent the next two years touring the country. It was when he was opening a bank account for the band in Denver that he was hired as a teller (after agreeing to cut his shoulder-length blonde hair twice), and so began a forty-year career in the banking business. In 1985, he married Lisa Bouley, a court reporter, and they had two children who are also CU grads, Casey James and Shelby, who married Andrew Cer in 2019. Kelso's family all live in Colorado, and he and Lisa live in Loveland, Colorado. Kelso retired from his role as community bank president of ANB Bank in Loveland, Colorado, in December 2020.

Karen graduated from St. Anne's-Belfield School in Charlottesville, Virginia, in 1973 and attended the University of Colorado-Boulder, spending a year there before Kelso enrolled. She graduated in 1977 with a degree in communication sciences and earned a MA in speech/language pathology at the University of Northern Colorado in 1979 and a doctorate in education from the University of Denver in 1995. Karen married in 1977 and began her career as a speech/language pathologist and early childhood educator in Colorado public schools. In later years, she served on the faculty at universities in Colorado and Montana and also worked with education agencies in the US and abroad. She divorced in 1997 and in 1999 Karen received a USIA Fulbright appointment to Cyprus, where she lived for a year with her second husband, John "Jock" Schorger, his two daughters—Ashley, who visited from Colorado College, and Colleen—as well as Karen's three children from her first marriage, Mollie and twins, Alex and Abbey. Mollie, now a school psychologist, lives in Reno, Nevada, with her husband, Oren Fallon, and daughters, Ainsley and

Hadley. Abbey lives in Kona, Hawaii, with her husband, Devin Hume, and works as a program manager for the environmental non-profit "Waterspirit," based in New Jersey, and as the social media director for the television series *Everything Hawaii*. Alex, a musician, lives in Penrose, Colorado, with Kitty Colvin and tours with several bands—most recently, the Yawpers. Karen retired in 2019 after ten years of working as an educational consultant in Qatar, France, and Dubai, UAE. She and Jock live in Las Cruces, New Mexico, where Jock enjoys his woodworking business, *Desert Peaks Custom Woodworking*, and Karen spends time writing books such as A *Place Called Brighton* (2021) while continuing to engage in international consulting.

Paula (Kay) enrolled at St. Margaret's School for Girls in Tappahannock, Virginia, but within the year, she was expelled due to a variety of reasons, not the least of which was failing to follow the strict rules about (not) smoking, (not) entertaining boys in her room, and (not) traveling off-campus, specifically convincing several classmates to hitchhike to a rock concert in Norfolk. She was later admitted to West Nottingham Academy in Maryland, where she would attend summer school and graduate a year early. Paula married at age nineteen and two years later divorced Joseph Stonesifer, a classmate from the academy. She then married Thomas Dawe of Long Island, New York, and they settled in Marietta, Georgia, with their three children, Kaylin, Charlie, and Jake. A fourth child, Adrienne, was born in 1999 after Paula's divorce from Tom. Paula, who struggled for many years with alcoholism, died in Marietta, Georgia, from liver disease in 2010.

The twins, Earl and David, attended and later graduated from York Academy, about thirty minutes from Brighton in West Point, Virginia. Earl attended Shepherd College in West Virginia, majoring in business, and after graduation, he moved to Washington, DC, to work in banking. He married a college classmate in December 1984, and they settled in Kill Devil Hills, North Carolina, where he joined a mobile accounting service. His interests soon evolved into an office-based business which he owns, Econtrol Business Systems, now based in Richmond. Earl and his daughter, Rae, live in Mechanicsville, Virginia, and his son, Tony, and his wife Angelika live in Kill Devil Hills, North Carolina.

David attended DeVry University in Atlanta, Georgia, and worked for a time with the Federal Reserve in Washington, DC and later with the Virginia State Courts system in Richmond. Currently employed with Capital One in Richmond, he's also the executor of the Kelly estate. In 2001, he married Denise Valenza, who owns Nest Gifts, LLC, and they live in Maidens, Virginia, with their two children, Madison and Joe. David and Earl and their families were regular visitors to Brighton, especially to spend time fishing and to support Eva Jo as she continued to upgrade and maintain the property over the years.

For many years following Claude's death, Eva Jo rented out the front fields at Brighton to a local farmer who alternated crops of winter wheat, soybeans, and corn. In the summers, she offered the grassy meadows by the pond to a local veterinarian for his cows to graze. She remodeled the small outbuilding that was the original kitchen, which was in a separate building from the main house, as was common during colonial days to reduce the risk of house fires. The space was upgraded to an apartment for use by guests, although for a short time, Eva Jo rented it to a local King William High School science teacher who enjoyed fishing for bass in the pond. The original red barn was renovated in 2008, keeping most of the original timbers, and the earthen dam at the pond was widened in 2014 for safety and improved access to the southern portions of the property. She added a two-car attached garage to the east side of the house in 2005, which included an upper level for storage. With Earl's help, she redesigned and renovated the existing unattached garage in 2016, turning it into a multipurpose farm shop attached to the guest apartment, which has retained the oversized brick fireplace used for cooking in colonial times.

Figure 129. Barn remodel 2008. Eva Jo decided to renovate the old red barn at Brighton. (Source: Kelly family archive)

Figure 130. The new barn was renovated in 2008, and the crew was able to salvage and retain many of the old original timbers. (Source: Kelly family archive)

Figure 131. The barn crew with Eva Jo and the crew leader, Keith Liskey. (Source: Kelly family archive)

Figure 132. The original kitchen was in an outbuilding in the colonial days, to reduce the risk of fire to the main house. When Eva Jo remodeled the old kitchen into an apartment, she was able to retain the original brick fireplace. (Source: Kelly family archive)

Figure 133. The dining room at Brighton was updated several times, most recently in 2018. (Source: The Steele Group Sotheby's International Realty)

Figure 134. View of the pond from the dining room at Brighton. (Source: Alex Koshak)

Figure 135. Blue willow plate collection displayed in the dining room at Brighton. This collection belonged to Mrs. Howard L. Clark and was included in the estate purchase of Brighton by Dr. Claude Kelso Kelly in 1952. (Source: The Steele Group Sotheby's International Realty)

Figure 136. Living room at Brighton July 2020. (Source: The Steele Group Sotheby's International Realty)

Figure 137. Master Bedroom at Brighton July 2020. (Source: The Steele Group Sotheby's International Realty)

Eva Jo spent most of her adult life at Brighton. Accustomed to living alone in her later years, she was hesitant to move to a smaller home, even as the Kelly children encouraged her to sell the farm and do so. In 2011, they celebrated her eightieth birthday at Kelly's Ford, Virginia, with over one hundred friends and relatives. A few years later, in 2015, Eva Jo, suffering from memory loss and dementia and diagnosed with advanced Alzheimer's disease, agreed to move to the Covenant Woods Continuing Care Community in Mechanicsville. Following a stroke in November 2018, her health deteriorated, and she died February 1, 2019, at the age of eighty-seven. Having spent almost sixty years of her life as a Kelly, it's likely that she was the longest resident of the place known as Brighton.

Figure 138. Eva Jo Kelly reading the morning news. (Source: Kelly family archive)

Figure 139. Eva Jo Kelly at her 80th birthday celebration at Kelly's Ford, Virginia September 2011. (Source: Devin Hume)

Figure 140. Eva Jo and family at her 80th birthday celebration. Pictured from left to right, back row: Jock Schorger, Karen Kelly, Rae Kelly, David Kelly, Denise Kelly, Tony Kelly, Earl Kelly, Kelso Kelly, Lisa Kelly, Casey Kelly; front row: Abbey (Koshak) Hume, Joseph Kelly, Eva Jo Kelly, Madison Kelly, Shelby (Kelly) Cer. (Source: Devin Hume)

Figure 141. Eva Jo Kelly obituary in the Tidewater Review newspaper February 6, 2019. (Source: Kelly family archive)

Figure 142. Eva Jo Kelly and Claude Kelly gravestones with Joseph Kelly at Sharon Baptist Church Cemetery in King William, Virginia. (Photo; David Kelly)

In July 2020, the Kelly family listed Brighton for sale with the Steele Group Sotheby's International Realty for $1,650,000 ($5,302 per acre).[11,12] And so, the next chapter of A Place Called Brighton, one of the oldest homes and historic properties in King William County, and now over 270 years old, remains to be written.

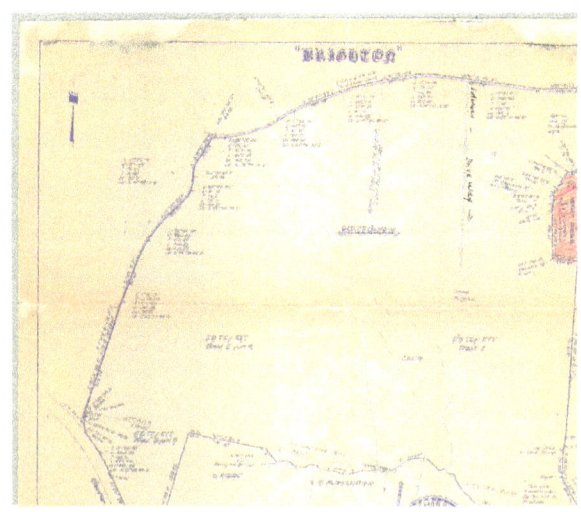

Figure 143. Survey of Brighton Farm by William F. Goodfellow (1973). (Kelly family archive)

Figure 144. Drone view of Brighton fields, the lane and the pond by Sotheby's. (Source: The Steele Group Sotheby's International Realty)

1. Abstract of Title Land Deeds of King William County Will Book 4, 283.
2. Abstract of Title Land Deeds of King William County Deed Book 72, 277.
3. Abstract of Title Land Deeds of King William County Deed Book 72, 279.
4. King William County Virginia Overall Notice of Change in Assessment Data (2021 Reassessment). https://www.kingwilliamcounty.us/DocumentCenter
5. Abstract of Title Land Deeds of King William County Deed Book 72, 277.
6. Jane Carroll Redd Dunford, *Recollections of My Father's Medical Practice in Hanover County*, an address presented to the Hanover County Historic Society, November 1991.
7. Mechanicsville Medical Center Family Practice, http://www.mechanicsvillemedicalcenter.com/
8. Mechanicsville Recreation Center, http://www.mechanicsvillepool.com/index.html
9. Grundman, Adolph H. (1972) Dissertation "*Public School Desegregation in Virginia from 1954 to the Present*," Wayne State University, https://digitalcommons.wayne.edu/cgi/viewcontent.cgi?article=1951&context=oa_dissertations
10. Richmond Times-Dispatch, September 2, 1956, 1.
11. Sotheby's International Realty Exclusive, https://www.sothebysrealty.com/eng/sales/detail/180-l-3708-y7rv6h/1600-upshaw-road-aylett-va-23009
12. 1600 Upshaw Road, Aylett VA, Sotheby's Realty, https://www.youtube.com/watch?v=77uhm-3E1Uo&feature=youtu.be

PHOTO EPILOGUE
The Kelly Family at Brighton

Figure 145. The ten-acre pond stretches along the southern boundary of the property at Brighton. Dr. Claude Kelly built the spring-fed pond that flows into Aylett Creek in 1958. All of the Kelly children learned to swim among the lily pads. They spent countless hours fishing, canoeing and enjoying the birds and other wildlife attracted to the solitude of Brighton pond. (Kelly family archive)

" For as long as I can remember the pond at Brighton was a highlight for family and friends alike. As children, we spent hours along the shore catching turtles and tadpoles, always on the lookout for copperheads and water moccasins. Over the years, we observed the work of the beavers as they decimated trees to construct their dam on the far side of the pond. We marveled at the diversity of birds, including great blue herons, osprey, eagles and endless flocks of geese who frequently settled on the cool, dark water. In the hot and humid summers the lily pads multiplied in vast patches, but we waded in and swam *anyway, squealing whenever we encountered one of the hundreds of cold springs on our way to dive off the homemade wooden float. We often shared the cool water with the black angus cows who came for a drink. We raced from one shore to the other in canoes and small skiffs, paddles cutting through the lily pads, flush with yellow blossoms. We fished, endlessly, from dawn to dusk, and the fish stories grew as we did, taller and more vivid each year. There are many unforgettable moments, such as the night Eva Jo woke me to help her paddle out in the boat to unclog the log encrusted overflow during a raging thunderstorm, as the water rose higher and threatened to break through the dam; the faceoff on the road across the dam between a wild turkey and a young deer (the deer eventually backed away); the morning mist on the water in the spring and the flakes of snow settling in patches along the shoreline that never fully froze in the winter. Even as we grew up and created stories and drama and families of our own, the pond remained a constant, always there as a peaceful place to return to and relive our youth."*

Figure 146. David and his 8-pounder citation fish and a 3-pounder caught in the pond at Brighton on a 100-degree day with cousin, Ben Harmon. (Kelly family archive)

Figure 147. Tony's catch of the day. (Kelly family archive)

Figure 148. David and his stringer of fish in the early 1980s. (Kelly family archive)

A PLACE CALLED BRIGHTON

Figure 149. Tony and another big fish. (Kelly family archive)

Figure 150. Earl's fish caught from the boat. (Kelly family archive)

Figure 151. David and Joe fishing from the old pier. (Kelly family archive)

Figure 152. Earl and Joe fishing from the shore. (Kelly family archive)

Figure 153. David fishing while Rae and Madison enjoy swimming (2011). (Kelly family archive)

Figure 154. Joe, Madison, Rae and Tony swimming in the pond. (Kelly family archive)

Figure 155. A friend of Earl's, Jennifer Cantrell, with a good catch for the day. (Kelly family archive)

Figure 156. Earl and another big one. (Kelly family archive)

Figure 157. Eva Jo and her catch for the day. (Kelly family archive)

Figure 158. Joe and his 22" prize catch. (David Kelly)

Figure 159. Joe poses with his Virginia 8-pounder citation fish. (David Kelly)

Figure 160. Rae, Madison and Abbey fishing from the old pier. (Kelly family archive)

Figure 161. Abbey and Madison looking for tadpoles along the shore. (Kelly family archive)

Figure 162. Rae fishing from the old pier. (Kelly family archive)

Figure 163. Rae and her catch of the day. (Kelly family archive)

Figure 164. Mollie and Abbey on the pier during summer lily pad season. (Kelly family archive)

Figure 165. David fishing in the lily pads. (Kelly family archive)

Figure 166. Upgrading and redoing the dam. (Earl Kelly)

Figure 167. Earl fishing in 2012. (Kelly family archive)

Figure 168. Jock fishing at Brighton from the new pier 2018. (Karen Kelly)

Figure 169. Jock and his catch of the day. (Karen Kelly)

Figure 170. Jock cleaning fish at the fish cleaning station at Brighton. (Karen Kelly)

Figure 171. Casey and his 21.5" bass. (Shelby Cer)

Figure 172. Casey and Kelso on the new dam with the catch of the day. (Shelby Cer)

Figure 173. David, Joe and Jock fishing from the boat. (Karen Kelly)

Figure 174. Fishing from the bass tracker boat with Jock, Joe and David. (Karen Kelly)

Figure 175. Eva Jo with Tony and Rae in the boat. (Kelly family archive)

Figure 176. Rae picking daffodils in the front yard at Brighton. (Kelly family archive)

Figure 177. Cows enjoying the cool waters of Brighton Pond. (David Kelly)

Figure 178. Deer grazing in the back field by the pond. (Jock Schorger)

Figure 179. Measuring the catch. (Kelly family archive)

Figure 180. Pond lily pads in the fall. (Kelly family archive)

Figure 181. Snow on the pond. (Kelly family archive)

Figure 182. Earl, Tony and Rae on the pony at Brighton. (Kelly family archive)

Figure 183. Mollie, Abbey and Alex in front of the English walnut tree in the front yard at Brighton. (May 2001). (Karen Kelly)

Figure 184. Karen and Jock in the back yard at Brighton June 2012. (Kelly family archive)

A PLACE CALLED BRIGHTON

Figure 185. Karen and Eva Jo in the back yard at Brighton 2011. (Kelly family archive)

Figure 186. Nate and Alex driving the Jocart in the lane at Brighton. (Kitty Colvin)

Figure 187. Proud parents David and Denise with Madison in the front yard at Brighton May 2019. (Kelly family archive)

Figure 188. Madison Kelly celebrating her High School graduation May 2019. (Kelly family archive)

Figure 189. Joe, Karen and Jock waving from the boat. (David Kelly)

Figure 190. Drone View from the southern boundary of Brighton. (The Steele Group Sotheby's International Realty)

List of Figures

1. Cover Photo: Brighton
2. Dedication Photo: Karen and her father, Dr. Claude Kelso Kelly
3. About the Author Photo: Karen and her family
4. Custom Map: King William County and location of Brighton

INTRODUCTION

5. Photo: Brighton, drone view June 2020
6. Photo: The Lane and Brighton Bullheads
7. Photo: Single Black Angus Bullhead
8. Photo: King William County Courthouse
9. Photo: King William County Courthouse
10. Photo: King William County Burned Records
11. Photo: House with pond reflection

CHAPTER ONE

12. Figure: Counties in Virginia in 1702
13. Photo: Cockacoeske Statue, Virginia Women's Museum
14. Figure: Map of Virginia by John Smith 1612
15. Figure: Herman Map 1670
16. Figures: Early Chickahominy/Mattaponi Indian Reservation
17. Figure: Three- mile buffer zone of Mattaponi Village in Aylett

CHAPTER TWO

18. Photo: Living room at Brighton with pine wood floors
19. Photo: William Byrd II
20. Document: Letter from Ryland to Clark regarding Brighton research

A PLACE CALLED BRIGHTON

21. Photo: Warsaw
22. Photo: Brighton 1940s
23. Document: Brighton and local farms historic writeup by Ryland
24. Photo: Barn and outbuildings at Brighton
25. Figure: Sketch of Brighton property survey
26. Photo: Arbor in the backyard at Brighton
27. Figure: Central passage-house floorplan
28. Figure: The Center passage house
29. Photo: Brighton Center Hall
30. Photo: Brighton dormer bedroom
31. Photo: Brighton chimneys
32. Photo: Brighton living room window

CHAPTER THREE

33. Photo: Brighton front view
34. Document: History of Brighton according to land records
35. Photo: Silas Broaddus sale of Brighton
36. Photo: Portrait of Major Beverly Browne Douglas
37. Document: *A Place Called Brighton* burned records book 14, p. 275
38. Document: Bessie Douglas birth record
39. Document: BB Douglas Cownes purchase
40. Photo: Pumphouse
41. Photo: Road thru the fields

CHAPTER FOUR

42. Document: Lee's Rangers
43. Photo: Portrait of Captain Thomas Witt Haynes
44. Figure: Blackford 1865 Civil War engineer's map
45. Figure: Blackford 1865 Civil War map with Aylett and Haynes home at Brighton
46. Figure: Hotchkiss 1863 Map of King William County
47. Document: Deed of Trust Taylor to Upshaw 1930
48. Document: Deed of Trust Fleet to Upshaw 1922

49. Document: Deed of Trust Upshaw to Clark 1933
50. Document: Mrs. Clark Winter home Brighton
51. Photo: Horsehead hitching posts and field at Brighton
52. Photo: Horse hitching post and house
53. Document: Sketch of Brighton Farm
54. Photo: Dr. Kelly in the front yard at Brighton
55. Photo: Back of the house
56. Photo: Side of the house
57. Photo: Brighton vintage aerial view 1980

CHAPTER FIVE

58. Photo: Brighton Overhead view with red barn
59. Photo: Brighton Sky view with red barn
60. Photo: View of house from the lane
61. Photo: House with white fence
62. Document: Brighton Deed 9.29.1952
63. Document: Brighton abstract of title
64. Photo: Claude and Kitty with their mother, Cecelia
65. Photo: Claude and Kitty portraits
66. Photo: Cecelia Bee Cartwright
67. Photo: Cecelia Cartwright at Brighton
68. Photo: Gravestones: Martha and Eddie Kelly, Sharon Baptist Church Cemetery
69. Photo: Dr. Claude Kelso Kelly in navy uniform
70. Photo: Claude Kelly and medical students at MCV
71. Photo: Dr. Kelly in Navy whites
72. Photo: 1960 Dr. Kelly and staff at the Mechanicsville Medical Center
73. Photo: Dr. Wysor, Crowe, Kelly and doctors at the Medical Center
74. Photo: Kitty (Kelly) Smallwood and Cecelia Cartwright at Brighton
75. Photo: Cecelia Cartwright and her son Claude in the front yard at Brighton
76. Photo: Dr. K and his mother, Celia under the grape arbor in the

backyard at Brighton
77. Photo: Dr. Kelly and car in the front yard at Brighton
78. Photo: Dr. K. and dogs
79. Photo: Black Angus in the field at Brighton
80. Photo: Nettie Virginia Joyner
81. Photo: Nettie Joyner Kelly at Brighton
82. Photo: Nettie at age 16
83. Photo: Nettie Joyner in her middle school band uniform
84. Photo: Nettie Joyner's nursing school graduation class, St. Luke's Hospital June 1953
85. Photo: Nettie and Claude at her graduation from Nursing School 1953
86. Photo: Claude and Nettie's wedding 1953
87. Photo: Claude, Nettie and Chainey at their wedding
88. Photo: Claude, Nettie, Merle and Chainey at their wedding
89. Photo: Claude and Nettie wedding party one
90. Photo: Claude and Nettie Wedding party two
91. Photo: Claude and Nettie wedding day in the car
92. Photo: Just married 1953
93. Photo: Dr. Kelly, Uncle Vernon and Chainey playing horseshoes in the backyard
94. Photo: Dr. Kelly and son Claude, Jr. 1954
95. Photo: Karen and Kelso in the pool
96. Photo: Claude, Jr. Karen and Paula XMAS 1956
97. Document: Herbert Kelly and Nettie Obituary 1957
98. Photo: Claude, Jr. (Kelso) on his new tractor in the front yard at Brighton
99. Photo: Claude, Jr. and Karen one month after their mother's death in 1957
100. Photo: Dr. Kelly and Eva Jo Liskey
101. Photo: Eva Jo Liskey
102. Photo: Eva Jo Liskey Kelly
103. Photo: Dr. Kelly and Eva Jo eating crabs
104. Photo: Dr. Kelly and Eva Jo at Brighton

105. Photo: Dr. Kelly, Eva Jo and family 1961
106. Photo: Kelly family 1964
107. Photo: Dr. Kelly and Eva Jo in the side yard 1965
108. Photo: Twins and tractor in the yard
109. Photo: Kelly twins and Dr. Kelly in the basement at Brighton
110. Photo: Dr. Kelly with Paula, Karen and the twins in the front yard at Brighton
111. Photo: Kelly kids on the monkey bars in the front yard at Brighton
112. Photo: Dr. Kelly obituary 1965
113. Photo: Claude, Jr., Paula and Karen celebrating Claude Jr.'s birthday in the basement at Brighton
114. Photo: Claude and Nettie gravestones
115. Photo: In Memory of Dr. Kelly
116. Photo: Basement dinner with the Eubanks and Aunt Kitty
117. Photo: Kelso, Karen, Earl and David at the Mechanicsville pool
118. Photo: Miss Lizzie and grandchildren in Ivor
119. Photo: Bullhead and kids in the pony cart
120. Photo: Kelly kids in the lane with pony cart
121. Photo: Kelly kids with Eliabeth Garlick's family
122. Photo: Fishing at Brighton
123. Photo: Kelso, Vernon, Lee and Steve Liskey
124. Photo: Kelly kids with the Smallwood and Gibson families at Brighton
125. Photo: Playing touch football in the backyard
123. Photo: Kelly kids and pyramid in the front yard
127. Photo: Smallwood family, Grandmother Cartwright and Kelly kids
128. Photo: Kelso squirrel hunting at Brighton
129. Photo: Barn remodel 2008
130. Photo: Barn new
131. Photo: Barn remodel crew
132. Photo: Original kitchen chimney
133. Photo: Dining room
134. Photo: View from the dining room

135. Photo: Blue willow collection in the dining room
136. Photo: Living Room at Brighton
137. Photo: Master bedroom at Brighton
138. Photo: Eva Jo Kelly reading the paper
139. Photo: Eva Jo Kelly at her 80th birthday celebration at Kelly's Ford, VA
140. Photo: Eva Jo Kelly and family at her 80th birthday celebration September 2011.
141. Photo: Eva Jo Kelly obituary in Tidewater Review newspaper
142. Photo: Eva Jo Kelly and Claude Kelly Gravestones with Joe Kelly 2019
143. Document: Survey of Brighton Farm 1973
144. Photo: Sotheby's Drone photo of Brighton 2020

Photo Epilogue: The Kelly Family at Brighton

145. Photo: House pond reflection
146. Photo: David and his 8-pounder citation fish and a 3-pounder caught in the pond at Brighton on a 100-degree day with cousin, Ben Harmon (Kelly family archive)
147. Photo: Tony's catch of the day (Kelly family archive)
148. Photo: David and his stringer of fish in the early 1980s (Kelly family archive)
149. Photo: Tony and another big fish (Kelly family archive)
150. Photo: Earl's fish caught from the boat (Kelly family archive)
151. Photo: David and Joe fishing from the old pier (Kelly family archive)
152. Photo: Earl and Joe fishing from the shore (Kelly family archive)
153. Photo: David fishing while Rae and Madison enjoy swimming (2011) (Kelly family archive)
154. Photo: Joe, Madison, Rae and Tony swimming in the pond (Kelly family archive)
155. Photo: A friend of Earl's, Jennifer Cantrell, with a good catch for the day (Kelly family archive)

156. Photo: Earl and another big one (Kelly family archive)
157. Photo: Eva Jo and her catch for the day (Kelly family archive)
158. Photo: Joe and his 22" prize catch (David Kelly)
159. Photo: Joe poses with his Virginia 8-pounder citation fish (David Kelly)
160. Photo: Rae, Madison and Abbey fishing from the old pier (Kelly family archive)
161. Photo: Abbey and Madison looking for tadpoles along the shore (Kelly family archive)
162. Photo: Rae fishing from the old pier (Kelly family archive)
163. Photo: Rae and her catch of the day (Kelly family archive)
164. Photo: Mollie and Abbey on the pier during summer lily pad season (Kelly family archive)
165. Photo: David fishing in the lily pads (Kelly family archive)
166. Photo: Upgrading and redoing the dam (Earl Kelly)
167. Photo: Earl fishing in 2012 (Kelly family archive)
168. Photo: Jock fishing at Brighton from the new pier 2018 (Karen Kelly)
169. Photo: Jock and his catch of the day (Karen Kelly)
170. Photo: Jock cleaning fish at the fish cleaning station at Brighton (Karen Kelly)
171. Photo: Casey and his 21.5" bass (Shelby Cer)
172. Photo: Casey and Kelso on the new dam with the catch of the day (Shelby Cer)
173. Photo: David, Joe and Jock fishing from the boat (Karen Kelly)
174. Photo: Fishing from the bass tracker boat with Jock, Joe and David (Karen Kelly)
175. Photo: Eva Jo with Tony and Rae in the boat.
176. Photo: Rae picking daffodils
177. Photo: Cows enjoying the cool waters of Brighton Pond (David Kelly)
178. Photo: Deer grazing in the back field by the pond (Jock Schorger)
179. Photo: Measuring the catch (Kelly family archives)
180. Photo: Pond lilypads in the fall (Kelly family archives)

181. Photo: Snow on the pond (Kelly family archives)
182. Photo: Earl, Tony and Rae on the pony at Brighton (Kelly family archive)
183. Photo: Mollie, Abbey and Alex in front of the English walnut tree in the front yard at Brighton (May 2001) (Karen Kelly)
184. Photo: Karen and Jock in the back yard at Brighton June 2012 (Kelly family archive)
185. Photo: Karen and Eva Jo in the back yard at Brighton 2011 (Kelly family archive)
186. Photo: Nate and Alex driving the Jocart in the lane at Brighton (Kitty Colvin)
187. Photo: Proud parents David and Denise with Madison in the front yard at Brighton May 2020 (Kelly family archive)
188. Photo: Madison Kelly after her High School graduation May 2020 (Kelly family archive)
189. Photo: Joe, Karen and Jock waving from the boat (David Kelly)
190. Photo: Drone View from the southern boundary of Brighton

Bibliography

1600 Upshaw Road, Aylett, VA, Sotheby's Realty, https://www.youtube.com/watch?v=77uhm-3E1Uo&feature=youtu.be

Abstract of Title Land Deeds of King William County (completed for Dr. Claude Kelso Kelly 1952). Deed Books, 2,7,9,14,15, 23,34,37,40,45,46,47,49,50,72. Will Book 4.

Atkinson, Dorothy. (1990) King William County in the Civil War, Along Mangohick Byways. Heritage Books, Inc., MD.

Bagby, Alfred. (1908) *King and Queen County*, Virginia. Neale Pub. Co. (Thomas N. Walker of the Walker Family by R. H. Land), https://books.google.com/books?id=3uzatQEACAAJ&pg=PA354-IA1&source=gbs_selected_pages&cad=2#v=onepage&q&f=false

Ball, Bonnie. (1978) Dr. Thomas Walker, *Historical Sketches of Southwest Virginia*. The Historical Society of Southwest Virginia, publication 12, 5–9. http://sites.rootsweb.com/~vahsswv/historicalsketches/walker%20drthomas.html

Bearss, Sara B. "Beverley Browne Douglas (1822–1878)," *Dictionary of Virginia Biography*, Library of Virginia (1998–) published 2016, http://www.lva.virginia.gov/public/dvb/bio.asp?b=Douglas_Beverley_Brown

Binford, J. H. (1915) "Snowbound in King William." *The Virginia Journal of Education*. Vol. 8.

Blackford, B. L. (1865) *Map of King William County*, VA. Confederate States of America. Army Dept. of Northern Virginia. Chief Engineer's Office [S.l.: Chief Engineer's Office, D.N.V] [Map] Retrieved from the Library of Congress. https://www.loc.gov/item/gvhs01.vhs00351/.

Bradbury, Eugene, Major. "*Historic American Buildings Survey*," Hillsborough, King and Queen County, https://cdn.loc.gov/master/pnp/habshaer/va/va1300/va1324/data/va1324data.pdf

Broaddus, Andrew. (1888) A History of the Broaddus Family: from the time of the settlement of the progenitor of the family in the United States down to the year 1888, 41, https://archive.org/details/historyofbroaddu00broa/page/40/mode/2up

Byrd, William. "A *Progress to the Mines in the Year* 1732 (142–143), published as part of "The Westover Manuscripts" in 1841, https://docsouth.unc.edu/nc/byrd/menu.html

Central-passage house, https://en.wikipedia.org/wiki/Central-passage_house

Chataigne's Virginia Gazetteer and Classified Business Directory 1888–1889. King William County, https://www.newrivernotes.com/topical_business_1888_chataigne_gazetteer.htm#KingWilliam

Clarke, Peyton Neale. (1897) Old King William homes and families: An account of some of the old homesteads and families of King William County, Virginia, from its earliest settlement, 7. Louisville, J. P. Morton and Co., https://archive.org/details/oldkingwilliamho00clar/page/6/mode/2up

Colonial Land Office Patents 1623–1774. Library of Virginia, https://www.lva.virginia.gov/public/guides/opac/lonnabout.htm

Conolly, B. *King William County Virginia Records 1702–1806, Record Books 1–5 including surviving fragments.* (2006) Formatted for e-book 2017 (Iberian Publishing). New Papyrus Publishing: Athens, Georgia.

Courtney, Giles C. (Elizabeth Spotswood Hill) (1905) *The Hill Family of Virginia.*

Cumming, William P. "Early Maps of the Chesapeake Bay Area: Their Relation to Settlement and Society," in David B. Quinn, ed., *Early Maryland in a Wider World* (Detroit: Wayne State University Press, 1982), 281–283; Ben C. McCary, John Smith's Map of Virginia (Williamsburg: Virginia 350th Anniversary Celebration Corporation, 1957), 1–3.

Cumming, William P., *The Southeast in Early Maps*, 3rd ed. (Chapel Hill: The University of North Carolina Press, 1998), 77; McCary, John Smith's Map of Virginia, 7; Verner, "*The First Maps of Virginia*," 9–10, https://www.lva.virginia.gov/public/guides/rn28_johnsmith.pdf

Douglas, Beverly B. https://en.wikipedia.org/wiki/Beverly_B._Douglas

Douglas family Bible records, Library of Virginia, http://image.lva.virginia.gov/Bible/32870/index.html?_ga=2.112238084.1873765329.1606066455-731966405.1598729338

Dunford, Jane Carroll Redd. (1991) *Recollections of My Father's Medical Practice in Hanover County*, an address presented to the Hanover County Historic Society on November 17, 1991.

Edwards, Bibb. (2012) *Our Courthouse Fires*. King William Historical Society.

Edwards, Bibb. (2015) Records recovered (KHS) *From the Ashes: King William County Burned Records*, https://kingwilliamhistory.org/wp-content/uploads/2018/11/news_2015_04.pdf

Elliott and Nye's Virginia Directory and Business Register. (1852) King William County, New River Notes. *Historical and Genealogical Resources for the Upper River Valley of North Carolina and Virginia*, https://www.newrivernotes.com/topical_business_1852_elliott_nye_directory.htm#

Farrell, Cassandra. (compiled 2007) *Virginia Discovered and Described: John Smith's Map of Virginia and its Derivatives*. Research notes, 28. Virginia Department of Historic Resources. The Library of Virginia, Richmond, https://www.lva.virginia.gov/public/guides/rn28_johnsmith.pdf

Fisher, Therese A. (1995; 2006) *Vital Records of Three Burned Counties: 1680–1860*. Heritage Books, Inc.: Westminster, MD.

Fleet, Beverly. (1988) *Virginia Colonial Abstracts*, 343. Baltimore, MD: Clearfield Company, Inc.

Foster, Gerald. (2004) *American Houses*, 94–95, Houghton Mifflin, https://archive.org/details/americanhousesfi00fost/page/94/mode/2up

Grundman, Adolph H. (1972) Dissertation "*Public School Desegregation in Virginia from 1954 to the Present*," Wayne State University, https://digitalcommons.wayne.edu/cgi/viewcontent.cgi?article=1951&context=oa_dissertations

Grymes, Charles A. "Acquiring Virginia Land by Headright," *virginiaplaces.org*

Harris, Malcolm H. (1977) Old New Kent County [Virginia] Some account of the planters, plantations, and places. Vol II, 845. King William County, West Point, VA.

Hill, Thomas T.H. Record of the Officers of KW County, VA, Virginia Historical Society; 1860 Census King William County.

Herrman, Augustine. 1621 Or, Henry Faithorne, and Thomas Withinbrook, *Virginia and Maryland as it is planted and inhabited this present year*. [London: Augustine Herrman and Thomas Withinbrook, 1673] Map. The Library of Congress, https://www.loc.gov/item/2002623131/

History and Old Homes of King William County, http://genealogytrails.com/vir/kingwilliam/county_history.html

Hotchkiss, J., Grant, J., Barrows, A. S., et al. (1863) *Map of King William County*, VA. [Map] Retrieved from the Library of Congress, http://hdl.loc.gov/loc.gmd/g3883k.cwh00042

King William County Historical Society, http://kingwilliamhistory.org/category/kwchs-projects/page/2/

King William Historical Society Newsletter October 1985. Bulletin Number 12.

King William County Virginia Overall Notice of Change in Assessment Data (2021 Reassessment), https://www.kingwilliamcounty.us/DocumentCenter/View/556/KWC-SALES-RATIO-STUDY-2021-REASSESSMENT?bidId=

King William County Virginia Records Land Transactions, Burned Records Files 1702–1884. Book 8, 27–28, King William County Historical Society.

King William County Virginia Records Land Transactions, Burned Records Files 1702–1884. Book 13, i141–144, King William County Historical Society.

King William County Virginia Records Land Transactions, Burned Records Files 1702–1884. Book 14, 275, King William County Historical Society.

King William County Land Records. Deed Book 15, i281.King William County Burned Records Microfilm. Library of Virginia, https://www.lva.virginia.gov/public/local/results_all.asp?CountyID=VA145

King William County Virginia, https://genealogyresources.org/King_William.html

Land Records of King William County. Deed Book 16, i421. King William County Burned Records Microfilm. Library of Virginia.

Land Tax Records of King William County 1782–1926, Reel 164-2050. Library of Virginia, https://www.lva.virginia.gov/public/guides/landTax-locality.asp?localityID=VA145

Library of Virginia. (2017) *Lost Records Localities: Counties and Cities with Missing Records*. Research Notes Number 30, https://www.lva.virginia.gov/public/guides/rn30_lostrecords.pdf

McIlwaine, H. R. and Kennedy et al. eds. (1905–1915) *Journal of the House of Burgesses*. 13 volumes. Richmond: Library of Virginia. 1695–1702, 349, 358. As cited in *Mattaponi Indian Reservation, King William County, Virginia* (October 2017). College of William and Mary Anthropological Research Report Series n.7 and Commonwealth of Virginia Research Report Series n. 23, 16, https://www.pocahontaslives.com/uploads/6/7/2/9/6729327/mattaponi_research_report_for_distribution.pdf

McMilliam, Jackson. (Jan. 7, 2015) "Historian tracks down original King William County documents dating back to 1702." *Tidewater Review*, https://www.dailypress.com/tidewater-review/va-tr-byline-kw-historical-society-documents-0107-20150106-story.html

Mechanicsville Medical Center Family Practice, http://www.mechanicsvillemedicalcenter.com/

Mechanicsville Recreation Association, Inc., http://www.mechanicsvillepool.com/index.html

Nugent, Nell Marion. *Cavaliers and Pioneers: Abstracts of Virginia Land Patents and Grants, 1623–1782*. 8 vols and supplement (vols. 4–8 published by the Virginia Genealogical Society, Dennis Hudgins, ed.) (Ref. F225 N841)

Nugent, Nell M. (1934) *Cavaliers and pioneers: A Calendar of Virginia land patents and grants* vol. 1. 1623–1800. Richmond: Dietz Press; reprinted Baltimore: Genealogical Publishing Company.

Official Site of the Mattaponi Indian Reservation, https://www.mattaponination.com/history.html

Page, Richard. (1883) *Genealogy of the Page Family in Virginia: Also a Condensed Account of the Nelson, Walker, Pendleton and Randolph Families.* New York: Jenkins & Thomas, Printers, https://archive.org/details/genealogypagefa00pagegoog/page/n224/mode/2u

Pearson, Sally. Commissioner of Revenue. King William County Property Assessment 2014.

Pendleton, Edmund, https://en.wikipedia.org/wiki/Edmund_Pendleton

Pendleton Family, http://freepages.rootsweb.com/~janet/genealogy/Pendleton.html

Richmond Times-Dispatch, September 2, 1956, 1.

Richmond Times-Dispatch, Obituary November 7, 1903.

Ruffin, Edmund (Ed.). (1841) Byrd, William (author). The Westover Manuscripts: Containing the History of the Dividing Line Betwixt Virginia and North Carolina; A Journey to the Land of Eden, A. D. 1733; and A Progress to the Mines. Written from 1728 to 1736. Petersburg: Edmund and Julian, Pub.

Ryland, Elizabeth. (1935) Personal Communication. History of Brighton According to Land Records." Presented to Mrs. Howard L. Clark, owner of Brighton.

Ryland, Elizabeth Hawes. (1935) Personal communication (letter) to Mrs. Howard L. Clark. King William County Land Office Records. Virginia State Archives. Book 9, 554.

Ryland, Elizabeth Hawes. (1935) Personal Communication to Mrs. Howard L. Clark describing King William County plantation homes and properties, including Brighton.

Ryland, Elizabeth Hawes. (1935) "Pamunkey Neck: The Birth of a Virginia County," *The Virginia Magazine of History and Biography*, Vol. 50, No. 4 (Oct. 1942), 321–333, Published by Virginia Historical Society

Ryland, E. H. (1955) King William County Virginia from Old Newspapers and Files. Richmond, VA: Dietz Press.

Sharon Baptist Church, King William, VA. http://www.interment.net/data/us/va/kingwm/sharon/index.htm (gravestones at Sharon Baptist Church)

Sotheby's International Realty Exclusive, https://www.sothebysrealty.com/eng/sales/detail/180-l-3708-y7rv6h/1600-upshaw-road-aylett-va-23009

Stantec (July 24, 2014). Figure 21. Brighton (c. 1765; VDHR #050-0007), 1600 Upshaw Road, View Looking Southeast 6.4. (*An Architectural Survey of King William County Cost Share 2014*)

Strickland, King, and McCartney. (2019) *Defining the Greater York River Indigenous Cultural Landscape (ICL)*, St. Mary's College of Maryland and the National Park Service (NPS), https://chesapeakeconservancy.org/wp-content/uploads/2020/02/York-ICL-Final.pdf

Survey of Hanover Historic Resources (1992). https://www.dhr.virginia.gov/pdf_files/SpecialCollections/HN-019_Survey_Historic_Resources_Hanover_PH_I&II_1992_LCA_report.pdf

The Bulletin of the King William County Historical Society (October 1979, no. 6). *Lee's Rangers*.

Upton, Dell. (1988) New Views of the Virginia Landscape. *The Virginia Magazine of History and Biography* 96, no.4:403–47, as cited in *An Architectural Survey of King William County* (Cost Share 2014) Stantec Consulting Services, Formerly CRI (July 24, 2014), 5.22.

Virginia Department of Education. *Virginia's First People: Upper Mattaponi Indian Tribe* http://www.doe.virginia.gov/instruction/history/virginias-first-people/today/upper-mattaponi/index.shtml

Virginia Department of Historic Resources (VDHR), https://www.dhr.virginia.gov/

Virginia Guide to the Old Dominion. (1992) Compiled by Workers of the Writers' Program of the Work Projects Administration in the State of Virginia. Virginia State Library and Archives. Tour 20 http://xroads.virginia.edu/~Hyper/VAGuide/TOUR20.html

Virginia History Series 6-7. (2007) *Life, Growth & Development in the Virginia Colonies (1700-1760). 21 Counties.* Slide 4, http://virginiahistoryseries.org/linked/unit%206.%20life.growth.development%20of%20va%20colony.slides.pdf.

Virginia Land and Properties, https://www.familysearch.org/wiki/en/Virginia_Land_and_Property

Virginia Quit Rent Rolls 1704. *The Virginia Magazine of History and Biography, Jul.* 1920, Vol. 28, No. 3 (Jul. 1920), 207–218. Published by: Virginia Historical Society Stable: https://www.jstor.org/stable/4243771

Vogt, John. (2011) King William County, VA 1810 Substitute Census [Abstracts from the 1810 Personal Property Tax List], https://heritagebooks.com/products/king-william-county-va-1810-substitute-census

Ward, Roger. (1998) 1815 Directory of Virginia Landowners. Vol. 3 eastern Region. Iberian Pub. Co: Athens, GA.

Weaver, Jeffrey. (1998) 1782 King William County, Virginia Personal Property Tax List. Government Tax Files. New River Notes. https://www.newrivernotes.com/neighboring_kingwilliam_enumerations_1782_personalpropertytax.htm

William and Mary Quarterly vol. 18, No. 4, Oct. 1938.

William and Mary Quarterly, Historical Magazine, Volume II, published 1893–94. Editor: Lyon G. Tyler, M.A., LL.D. Whittet and Shepperson, Printers: Richmond, Virginia.

Zontine, Patricia. (April 2009) Dr. Thomas Walker (1714–1794). Jefferson Library. Monticello, https://www.monticello.org/sites/library/exhibits/lucymarks/lucymarks/bios/drthomaswalker.html

www.ingramcontent.com/pod-product-compliance
Lightning Source LLC
Chambersburg PA
CBHW061200070526
44579CB00009B/80